The ABC's of THC and CBD

A Joint Study of the Cannabis Plant and the Cannabinoid Revolution

Dr. Russell J. Zwanka

ISBN-13: 9798672730851

Hemp is Earth's number-one biomass resource; it is capable of producing 10 tons per acre in four months.
Jack Herer

When you smoke the herb, it reveals you to yourself.
Bob Marley

Also by Zwanka

The Store Walk: A Walk Through A Grocery Store in Today's Environment

Magic Mushrooms: Future Trend or One-Time Trip?

A Post Pandemic Store Walk

Pandemic Positivity: Turning a Pandemic into a Roadmap for a Positive Life

Food Forethought: 48 Healthy Food Tips for Navigating the Grocery Store

Simple Solutions to Make Customers Feel Like Your Supermarket is Their Supermarket

Ties That Bind: Inside the Extraordinary (sometimes knotty) Food Marketing Continuum

CBD Reality

A note from your professor

CBD Dreams

Public Speaking for Everyone

So, how do I do this Marketing thing?

Marketing in Today's Cuba

A Store Walk

Dr. Z's Guide to Grocery and Cooking and Cool Stuff Like That

Successfully Succinct Stage Speaking

A Marketing Manual for the Millennium

Category Management Principles

Customer Connectivity in Global Brands and Retailers

Requisite Reading for the Renaissance Retailer

Operating in the New Cuba

Food Retail Management Strategic Cases

Would You Shop Here if You Didn't Work Here?

Customers First. Profits Second.

About Dr. Z

Dr. Russell J. Zwanka is Director of the Food Marketing Program, and Professor of Category Management and Food Marketing, at Western Michigan University, one of the top Food Marketing programs in the world. Delivering high quality curriculum and applied food marketing skills, along with the Food Industry Research and Education Center, Western Michigan University endeavors to work with current stakeholders in the industry to provide real time solutions; while also helping educate the future leaders of the food industry. Zwanka has also previously taught Marketing Research, Personal Selling, Marketing Strategy, Food Marketing, Business Strategy, and Marketing Principles.

Having spent a career in the food industry before teaching, Dr. Z conceptualized and formed the Food Marketing Concentration at Siena College; as well as the Food Marketing Track at the State University of New York at New Paltz. Serving as the Chair of the Food Industry University Coalition (FIUC), Zwanka works with other universities teaching Food Marketing, to help educate the future of the food industry. The FIUC is made in part by the generosity of the National Grocers Association (NGA).

Dr. Z is CEO of Triple Eight Marketing, a retail consultancy- helping food organizations re-align around customer lifestyle and orientation. Dr. Z has led the merchandising, marketing, advertising, procurement, and all customer engagement areas for multiple food retail companies domestically and internationally.

Zwanka holds a Doctorate in International Business from ISM in Paris, France. He also holds a Master of Science in Management from Southern Wesleyan University, and a Bachelor of Science in Psychology from the University of South Carolina. Never stop learning....

Dr. Z can be followed at "Dr.Z@TEM888" on most social sites.

Table of Contents

CBD and THC

If you've read my previous two books on Cannabidiol (CBD), *CBD Dreams* and *CBD Reality*, the first book was written from a perspective of presenting research and information for a retailer to use in making product decisions; the second book was more of a focus on the consumer and how the consumer can wade safely into the CBD waters. In each of these books, Tetrahydrocannabinol (THC) was intentionally excluded from the discussion. Too much legal, too much stigma....too much too much! You had "weed people" and you had "CBD people". Never the two shall mix.

If you want to call this book the third part of the trilogy, this book is being written from the perspective we cannot ignore the overlap of all products from the cannabis plant. As further evidence is showing, this plant (herb....if you're Bob Marley) has some wondrous qualities. And, as research develops, the cannabinoids work so well together. It all boils down to how the cannabinoids and their terpenes interact with our CB1 and CB2 receptors in our Endocannabinoid System (ECS). It used to be simple, CBD only bonds with CB2 and THC bonds with both. It's not that simple anymore. The "entourage effect" is a real thing, where the individual parts are made stronger by the presence of their other cannabinoid and terpene friends.

This book is about a healthy solution for many of our issues, mostly stemming from sleep deprivation and inflammation. Mostly, though, this book is about a natural substance that can be used to replace the synthetic medications that are so willingly handed out by our medical professionals- and so easily covered by our insurance providers, not allowing an economically feasible way to break the synthetic cycle.

Welcome to the third book of the "Cannabis Trilogy"!

History Cannot be Ignored

It all started a few years ago. 8,000 BC, to be exact. Assuming you were probably not around in 8,000 BC, let's talk a little about what was going on at the time. There was this magical crop, one of the most productive and earth-cleansing crops ever, some say it was the perfect crop. A life saver of a plant. A plant that could save the trees, clean the air, be planted again and again and actually *help* the earth year over year. A perfect crop! If something like that were available today, especially with our focus on the ravages we have beset upon our environment, it would behoove us to jump all over it, right? Prop it up, praise it, support it at all levels of government, right?

Well, if you are feeling a sense of obligation from those words, a sense of wanting to do something to help this earth, something to put you closer in touch with this beautiful sphere we call home, *have we got a plant for you*! Hemp!

Uh oh….here we go….isn't that the stuff that gets you high? Well, yes and no. Hemp plants contain no more than .3 percent of tetrahydrocannabinol (THC), which is the widely popular psychoactive substance found in marijuana. To say it again, cannabis plants with .3 percent or less of THC are hemp. Cannabis plants with more than .3 percent THC are commonly reeferred (yes, that was intentional) to as marijuana.[1]

I'm asking you to change your mindset for this book. Instead of finding all the reasons why products labeled hemp (industrial hemp, when discussing cannabidiol (CBD)) are bad, let's look at the positives. And, whether you are a person with inflammation who is wondering if it is right for you, a retailer wondering if you should sell it, a consumer packaged goods company thinking you might want to produce it, or even a government trying to figure out what to do with it, you should be convinced by the end of this book of the beauty of this plant. We'll talk about THC, and it's interweaved connection to CBD, and the inability of many to separate the two substances. Think of hemp and THC as twins separated at birth. One becomes an all-healing bringer of goodness. The other one has all the healing powers of its twin, but has a little wild streak to it. The little sister that sneaks in a kiss while the big sister isn't looking. Neither one really harms you, but they function in society differently. And therein lies the rub, they're the same but different.

Hemp has been around how long?

Until the last one hundred years or so, hemp has been weaved into the fabric of society for as long as can be documented. In fact, there were hemp clothing remnants found in the Middle East dating back to the aforementioned 8,000 BC. More than likely, if the documented history is written on anything, it's actually written on hemp. The Chinese have been major producers of hemp from 28th century BC until the present day. In fact, almost 70% of the industrial hemp biomass used in CBD today comes from China. We'll talk later whether or not that is a good idea. For now, suffice it to say hemp has earned its place in history.[2]

Hemp was originally grown for textiles, primarily clothing, and it was for that reason hemp made it from China to Europe roughly 700 years ago (depending upon when you're reading this book, I guess). China has the longest history with hemp cultivating, followed by France, Spain, Chile, and Russia. As with any wonder crop that actually helps the soil as it's repeatedly grown, multiple other uses became apparent. China, at roughly 200 BC found hemp to be particularly useful for paper making.[3] The oldest written documents are Buddhist texts from 2nd and 3rd centuries AD, primarily made of hemp. Think of how much heavier notebooks were when they were made of tablets....

Now, go a little further, and hemp rose to the forefront as a plant with healing abilities. Ancient remedies began to use hemp for arthritis, difficulty in childbirth, convulsions, dysentery, and insomnia. Sound familiar? Same benefits being touted in present day from both CBD and THC.

Progressing through history, hemp became a major economic crop in the middle ages, being used in food, drugs, paper, clothing, rope, etc. In fact, hemp is three times stronger than cotton and is resistant to salt water. In fact, the word "canvas" is derived from the word "cannabis". Inevitably, hemp made it to North America, and is said to have been grown in every state, at some point.

Unfortunately for hemp, harvesting was quite labor intensive, and the cotton gin helped cotton become the favored clothing crop. The hemp industry, especially in regards to clothing, was attacked on all sides. Not worrying about the environment, major petroleum-based synthetic textile companies took aim at hemp. New machines were developed that would have allowed hemp to compete, but the lobbying industry was quite convincing and the government began to add major excise taxes on hemp dealers; and then banned it altogether under the 1938 Opium and Narcotics Act.[4] As we said previously, hemp is inextricably connected to its wilder and crazier twin marijuana.

During World War II, the United States government lifted restrictions on hemp. Kind of like a redemption moment, hemp was used to help support the war effort, only to be placed back under the ban when the war ended. Thanks, but no thanks, hemp....appreciate your support and diversified ability to be used in paint, ink, varnish, paper, canvas, rope, money, food, textiles, brakes, clutches, plastics, and even being the fabric upon which was written the Declaration of Independence! You're still banned. Why? Well, of course, your twin....

Oh, say, can you THC!

Oh yeah, hemp's twin separated at birth. THC! First, let's get a little something straight. It's common to refer to THC as the "psychoactive part" of the cannabis plant. We should clarify. Psychoactive is defined as "a drug, or other substance, that affects how the brain works and causes changes in mood, awareness, thoughts, feelings, or behavior. Examples of psychoactive substances include alcohol, caffeine, nicotine, marijuana, and certain pain medicines. Many illegal drugs, such as heroin, LSD, cocaine, and amphetamines are also psychoactive substances."[5]   All cannabinoids from the cannabis plant, of which CBD and THC are two of them, impact mood, awareness, etc. THC has the ability to give you "the high". CBD can calm anxiety. Both impacts are psychoactive. Drinking a Red Bull can be psychoactive!

So, back to the wilder twin THC. How did this thing happen where a seemingly innocent cannabis plant can serve up two kids, both helpful, just one a little wilder? And, by the way, who just sees a plant and says, "Hey, I'd like to smoke that?". All good questions.

Cannabis plants are actually found in the wild, and not planted by Cheech and Chong. You can find cannabis plants growing wild in eastern Russia and western China, as well as other parts of Central Asia. But, as industrious humans, the wild plants were not quite strong enough for us, lacking in cannabinol (CBN) and THC; so, we developed a way to increase those levels. Because, hey, why have a plant if it's not loaded with THC, right? In defense of those who figured out how to increase and decrease cannabinoid levels (CBN, CBD, THC, CBG, etc. are all cannabinoids), the plant has been used for years to control or offset pain, inflammation, nausea, etc.[6] It wasn't just to "get high".

Let's take that statement and build a bit upon it. Take the "high" part out of the equation, and think in terms of medicinal purposes. The challenge for mankind has always been to find cures for our various health issues. Our bodies are great little machines for warding off viruses, bacteria, diseases, etc. When in equilibrium, our bodies are pretty awesome! And, as we will discuss further on in this book, our bodies are made to maintain equilibrium (called homeostasis) with our Endocannabinoid System (ECS). The same substances found in the cannabis plant (cannabinoids) are biologically produced in our bodies.

But, things go wrong. Our bodies cannot fight off everything. And, unfortunately, most illnesses and diseases involve pain. Whether it is chronic inflammation, short term pain, or even pain from bumping your head, the body needs help covering the pain. Remember, our bodies are made for "fight or flight", and covering pain is one way our body allows us to fight or get the heck out of there! Finding mind-altering substances to mask pain has been a goal the entire time man has existed. It just happens that some of these substances can be addictive, and impact our bodies in unique ways.

And here's where the road splits. Are you starting to see why CBD and THC are inseparable? Can you also start to see why cannabis can be lumped in with coca and opium poppy? For one thing, they have all been used by doctors to help control or cover pain in patients. Morphine drips in hospitals, cocaine in certain surgeries, cannabis in certain treatments. All useful for original intended purpose. All at varying addictive levels. Next, though, they do such a tremendous job covering the pain, many patients don't want it to ever end. And, then, when life just kind of sucks sometimes, going into "another world" with mind-altering substances is a choice made by many. Unfortunately, that choice can then become an addiction. Romanticize it, and you can call it "going inside my own head." A common phrase today.

Both cannabis and opioids are effective in pain management. But, while cannabis has never been linked to a death by lethal dosage, more than three out of five drug overdose deaths involve an opioid.[7] Add the legal availability of opioids through doctors, and the illegal availability (varies by state) of cannabis, and cannabis has gotten a bad rap here. In fact, the makers of synthetic opioids openly lobbied against cannabis! Of course they did.

A Changing of the Mind

When I first started studying cannabidiol CBD, I only wanted to study it so I could help guide the food industry in understanding this substance and in taking advantage of the growth opportunity. I specifically stated I was not advocating for CBD, only informing.

Much has progressed since my research began. Number one? As I've become more informed, I've become more convinced of the benefits. In fact, I'm almost 100% certain CBD can impact your life in a positive way. So, I've gone from neophyte to advocate.

CBD, it seems, is being touted by many as something that pretty much cures anything. Unfortunately, when claims of "curing everything" are offered to the public, there is a natural inclination to believe there is very little truth to any of the claims. In the way zealots are "crazy" or "fringy", great claims are followed by great skepticism- as they should be.

I'll be the first to admit, I saw the claims and felt similarly- there is no way this stuff works, right? But, fast forward a year, fast forward roughly 300 research pages written, 1000's of sources checked and double-checked, validation and fact-checking, 100's of in-person interviews, as well as trying it myself, and I am convinced CBD can be the answer to our dependency upon pharmaceuticals so easily prescribed by the nation's doctors. The following pages lay out the case for CBD, and maybe they will hopefully help convince our government to act quicker towards granting full legal status for all hemp-derived CBD products.

In the meantime, we have this inevitable crossover of people trying CBD and THC, and we need to add THC into the equation. Why? Because for many people, THC never left the discussion. I would state, for the record, focus in on only CBD and the race will pass you. You cannot solely research CBD and not take in THC, CBN, CBG, etc. Call it the "entourage effect" (which we will discuss later). Let's talk about the connections.

Tetrahydrocannabinol- The Wild Child

It seems THC has made a remarkable resurgence in popularity the last few years. A "war on drugs" tends to diminish the desire to try certain substances, when even an ounce could be called "trafficking"! Now that the difference between LSD and opium versus THC has been realized, the legalization of THC across the country and the world seems like an unstoppable wave. It starts with decriminalization, goes on to legalization for medical marijuana, and then to legalized recreational marijuana. The fact you could buy 151 proof Everclear legally, but not a bud of THC, has never really made sense.

We will not be talking too much about medical marijuana. If you are eligible for it, you probably know the benefits. We can leave it at that. Where we want to take the discussion is on the recreational side. As we stated, the popularity of THC is off the charts! Go stand outside a dispensary and watch the traffic flow. These places are crazy busy. The growth is staggering! By 2025, it is projected there will be $23B in marijuana sales in the United States alone. Led by....you guessed it, California.[8] There are roughly 28,000 legal marijuana businesses in the US, with the majority of the investment in growth occurring in 2016.[9]

The distribution of sales? Flower/ plant type makes up 54% of the sales, while edibles are broken into almost half being candy and roughly 17% being tinctures. Vape accounts for 7% of sales. Versus other substitutable type items, marijuana is roughly half that of alcohol, has exceeded tobacco, and is a third of the sales of painkillers.[10]

Why are people buying it? According to multiple surveys, roughly 55% are buying recreational marijuana to relax, 40% are using it to relieve stress or for social reasons, and 30% use it for anxiety or improving sleep. Almost all marijuana consumers see it as less dangerous than methamphetamine, heroin, cocaine, LSD, ecstasy, and opioids.[11]

One other study backed previous studies, with some additional findings, with 60% of respondents using CBD/THC for chronic pain and 34% using it for migraine pain. The most common delivery method in this study was vaping (41%), then topical (32%) and tincture (31%). Edibles and capsules were not far behind, at 27% and 26%, respectively. Most responded they were using CBD/THC because it was not as addictive, and had fewer side effects, than other drugs.[12]

The reasons for using CBD and THC are almost identical. As we've said before, these cannabinoids are inevitably connected. When you deliver the substance in the same forms, and it's used the same, you need to take in the total picture of the cannabis plant. And, when marijuana becomes legal in your state, the mix of sales of CBD and THC obviously is impacted. Usually in favor of THC.

So, is it legal? The answer? Who the heck knows! Keep this in mind, CBD is legal nationally, and the states get to determine if it's illegal. THC is illegal nationally, and the states get to choose if they want to legalize it. And, in case that was actually clear, there are five different combinations of legality: Completely legal, medically legal and decriminalized, medically legal only, decriminalized only, or totally illegal. Yes, decriminalized means exactly that….it's not legal, it's just not criminal. [13]

And who is buying it? According to one survey, 22% of those between 18-29 are using marijuana, 11% of those between 30-49 are using it, 12% between 50-64, and those over 65 are at 3%.[14]

To put it all together, we have one heck of a trend on our hands! And, as we have researched with CBD, the trend is almost identical between THC and CBD. Now, before we go to CBD, let's talk about some of the other up and coming trendy cannabinoids.

THC Culture

If anything hurts or helps, sways or discourages, THC use, it's the THC culture. As much as this book is about the similarities of THC and CBD and the rest of the cannabinoids, this is where THC sets its own course. The THC culture is strong! If you are going to partake in, or even sell, THC, understanding the culture and the terminology is key.

A few terms to understand:

Anandamide- As we try to understand why THC makes you feel heightened senses, makes you a bit off-balanced, and makes you crave cheeseburgers, we like to see what it's doing with our endocannabinoids in our brain. Anandamide is an endogenous cannabinoid (one our body makes) that is also called the "bliss molecule". The name derives from the Sanskrit *ananda*, which can be loosely translated as joy.[15] Anandamide was discovered by Dr. Raphael Mechoulam, when he was researching why certain human receptors bond so well to THC. He also, by the way, discovered THC.[16] Certain endogenous cannabinoids act as agonists to the CB1 and CB2 receptors.[17] In other words, they act as amplifiers of effect. This one makes bliss the primary feeling, and amplifies pleasurable activities such as sex and eating.

Dopamine- THC stimulates receptors that activate the brain's reward system, which then indicates to the brain to flood the body with dopamine. This release of dopamine contributes to the high most people experience with THC.[18] Dopamine and anandamide are quick release results, and do not last long. Thus, you eventually "come down".

The munchies- Okay, so that's not really a term, per se, more like a given. THC impacts the hippocampus and orbitofrontal cortex, which impair short term memory, task focus, and balance.[19] With those things out of the way, and with the reward system firing on all cylinders, the pleasure activities tend to become more pleasurable and more desirable. As mentioned before, eating is one of those activities. THC is like adding salt to life. It enhances the senses.

Greening out- If you are going to understand the culture, you need to understand what people are saying, right. You "green out" when you start to head the wrong way under the influence of THC.[20] It's either because you took too much, or you're just extremely uncomfortable with the process and the process of introducing THC to your body actually increases anxiety. It's not fatal, although it's been described as "that sucks".

Battery and cart- It's the vape pen, and is mostly a battery. In fact, they plug into the wall.[21] As opposed to passing the joint back and forth like Cheech and Chong would have encouraged, you can carry your own cartridge (cart) and attach it to anyone's battery. Much more sanitary.

Buds and flowers- The smokable part of the cannabis plant. You're not included stems, and the non-smokable components. Just the flower.[22]

Budtender- I hope you don't need a definition to know this one.

Bowl- The part of the pipe used to hold the flower. Some people get quite creative with their decorative bowls. Go to Seattle and there are thousands of bowls for sale as crafts.[23]

Dabs or BHO- Butane Hash Oil, where marijuana is dissolved in butane and results in a highly potent gooey substance which is consumed from a red hot surface.[24] Serious stuff!

Terpenes- These are the aromas that normally work together with substances to enhance effect. Terpenes are described quite often in the THC and CBD extraction process, and have a variety of types.[25]

Trichomes- The resin producing glands of the cannabis plant. It's where the THC, CBD, and other cannabinoids are produced.[26]

Dispensary- For anyone new to a legal state and wondering where everyone is purchasing their THC, this is where. Be prepared to not be anonymous. You go through security, check in at the front with an identification card (driver's license, usually), and wait to be called (post-COVID). Called forward by your budtender….

420- It's commonly known that April 20th (4/20) is called "weed day". Also, pretty much any day at 4:20, someone is bound to say, "Hey, guys, it's 4:20!". The origin has mystical stories of Hitler and/or Bob Dylan, but the most widely accepted story is the one of The Waldos, a group of five kids at San Rafael High School (California, of course) who would smoke weed behind the bleachers every day at 4:20.[27]

710- This is a new one, and not as commonly known outside the THC culture. July 10th (7/10) has become known as "oil day" (flip 710 upside down….), which gives those who partake in THC oils one more reason to partake.[28]

Sativa and Indica- Coming from *cannabis sativa* and *cannabis indica*, these two are two different species of cannabis. They have differing leaf and stalk length, etc. Some say indica is more calming and sativa is more energizing. Some say that's just anecdotal. What *is* known is that sativa has higher CBD levels and indica has higher THC levels.[29] Most of the time, you are purchasing hybrid product.

Ratios- As we have completed research in states where THC is recreationally legal, there has been a tremendous demand for ratio products. The ratio goes like this: CBD:THC, as in 1:0 is CBD only, 1:2 gives you more of the high, since THC is the dominant cannabinoid, and 1:1 has the optimal medicinal qualities without the anxiety that may come from the process of knowing you are taking THC.[30] The entourage effect is playing in here, as well, since you receive the entourage benefits from both CBD and THC, as well as the other cannabinoids.

Just wait a minute- Okay, so that's not really a term or phrase commonly used; but, it *is* a warning that comes from most regular users of THC (especially when discussing edibles). Take a little and wait, if you're not sure. Edibles tend to be quite potent and they take about 40-60 minutes to work through your digestion system. Remember the cartoon "These edibles ain't....", then they're flat on their back stoned?

These terms and clarifiers were mostly meant to cover some of the more unique aspects of the THC culture. The words weed, dope, bongs, etc. I did not think were necessary to cover, since they are so widely known. As with any list, I'm sure a new word or term popped up in the *Urban Dictionary* as I was writing this chapter.

The Other Cannabinoids

We've made much out of THC and CBD, as the most widely known cannabinoids. But, as the compounds and health impacts of the cannabis plant become more widely known, other cannabinoids are coming to the game and want to play along with their two better known siblings. Researchers are working to isolate various specific impacts of the cannabinoids, in order to pinpoint solutions for specific issues, like cancer, insomnia, IBS, etc. Here are a few of the rising stars of the cannabinoid family.

Cannabigerol- CBG is also known as the "Mother Cannabinoid". Both THC and CBD come from CBG. Most recreational consumers have not heard of CBG outside of California, but it does seem to show neuroprotective properties. Additionally, it shows positive impacts on inflammation, pain, nausea, cancer, and glaucoma.[31] Between CBG and CBN, these could be the next two big cannabinoids.

Cannabinol- CBN, as mentioned above, has a ton of groundswell support- especially in California. When THC degrades, it turns into CBN. But, CBN has been shown to be an excellent sedative and is one of the more popular cannabinoids for sleep.[32]

Cannabichromene- CBC has been shown to have outstanding impacts on bacteria, fungi, and also as an anti-depressant. CBC is the third most prevalent cannabinoid.[33]

Tetrahydrocannabivarin- THCV, on the recreational side, has been shown to give a clear-headed burst of energy and a psychedelic high. On the medical side, THCV has been shown to instrumental in controlling glycemic levels in diabetics, aiding in weight loss, and stimulating bone growth.[34]

Cannabidiolic Acid- CBDA is related to CBD, and is its acidic precursor. In some raw THC, CBDA is prevalent and does have some impacts on the body. In fact, in some studies, CBDA delivered anti-depressant effects 100 times more effective than CBD.[35]

There are over 115 cannabinoids discovered, so far, so we are just scratching the surface in identifying singularly focused positive impacts from each cannabinoid. Most of these substances do not give you the THC high, and most share the same underlying health benefits. When identifying a singular strain, it's more about what it does *even better* and not about what the others do worse.

So, what is legal?

The question of the day. Is this stuff legal? Instead of the first answer that comes to mind: "Who tf knows?", it depends.... The 2018 Farm Bill removed hemp from being recognized as a Schedule 1 controlled substance, where it had been placed due to its relationship to cannabis. Cannabis was placed in the same family of substances as heroin, LSD, and ecstasy. It had been commonly interpreted by the Drug Enforcement Agency (DEA) that anything hemp was also part of Schedule 1. Lumping them all in together is an easy way to let ignorance of facts drive legislation. After the 2018 signing of the Farm Bill, hemp-derived CBD was now considered legal.

The Food and Drug Administration (FDA), which is charged with regulating the food you ingest, saw companies were infusing food with a substance now considered legal. So, the FDA came right back in and said CBD-infused foods were still illegal. Cannot make health claims, cannot call it food, cannot cannot cannot.... Then, sporadically agencies would raid stores and remove all CBD products, due to their own interpretation of the laws. Then, the Transportation Security Agency (TSA) would seize anything and call it THC, because their detection devices could not tell the difference, and then some states started allowing hemp-derived products, just not ingestible....then then then! With a lack of leadership from the government, confusion still reigns. One bit of advice, you might just want to avoid traveling with CBD. Are you really going to be the pioneer who convinces a TSA officer that your product is legal? Just leave it at home. If you want, buy some when you land.

As of today, hemp is federally legal and the states can still interpret however they would like. On the flipside, THC is federally illegal, and the states are still interpreting however they would like. Cool! Thanks!

I am not interested in being embroiled inside the medical marijuana versus recreational marijuana battle. That's for someone else to argue for, or against. When you think of the benefits of the products from the cannabis plant, the government does its constituents a disservice by declaring a "war on drugs" against marijuana while allowing the Sackler family to make billions on opioids being fed to humans like candy with OxyContin.[36]

Both THC and hemp are members of the cannabis family, so they do share many characteristics. There is, however, a crucial difference between the two: the amount of psychoactive tetrahydrocannabinol (THC) each plant produces. While the substance called marijuana can contain up to 30% or more THC, CBD from hemp contains no more than 0.3% THC. Marijuana can get you "high", while hemp has such a low amount of THC, that it would be impossible to get high off it.[37]

When you see CBD sold, it comes in usually three forms: Isolate, Full Spectrum, and Broad Spectrum. For the purposes of this book, we will equate Full and Broad Spectrum. They're pretty much the same thing. We need to define the difference between "CBD Full Spectrum" and "CBD Isolate". CBD Full Spectrum contains all other cannabinoids found in the cannabis plant including CBN (Cannabinol), CBG (Cannabigerol), and THCV (Tetrahydrocannabivarin), to name a few. And yes, along with these cannabinoids, Full Spectrum CBD also contains trace amounts of THC (Tetrahydrocannabinol), but in very low concentrations (up to .3%), resulting in very minimal psychoactive stimulation. CBD Isolate is simply purified CBD that has been extracted from the cannabis plant and isolated from the other cannabinoids.[38] The natural next question is which one is the one I want? It was previously believed the CBD Isolate was more effective, but recent studies have shown Full Spectrum to be more effective. You might want to ask your doctor, but for the general population, CBD Full Spectrum is the most widely accepted form available. If you absolutely positively want to make sure there is no THC in your body, go with Isolate. As long as it's labeled correctly....

What Progress Has Been Made?

The majority of the CBD being sold today is either through natural and organic food stores, vape shops, or Amazon. There are some things you can do to ensure you can trust the label and the contents match, and we'll talk about those. Take the time to get to know the company before buying. Honestly, with Amazon's vetting process, I'm not so sure I would run to Amazon first to make a CBD purchase. The larger consumer packaged goods (CPG) companies have been averse to the potential negative stigma of CBD, so have been only hinting they want to enter the market. It's okay to sell you a can with 46 grams of sugar in it, but let's hold off on CBD.

The fact is, though, if the larger CPG companies would enter the marketplace, we would have *better* oversight and *clearer* regulation. The larger brands have more brand equity at stake. Nestle's brand equity versus High Dog CBD's is pretty apparent. Yes, in this case, we want regulation. The number of products being found labeled as CBD, but containing no CBD or too much CBD or exceeding the allowed level of THC, means we need the government to take control of the regulation of the contents- clearly defining sourcing and packaging regulations. To be labeled Organic is to follow a process. That's the type of regulation we need. Stop debating legality, and start regulating the contents to keep the public safe!

CVS and Walgreens have announced their intent to sell creams, sprays, roll-ons, lotions, and salves in 2,300 stores, over the counter. CVS in 800 of their stores (in California, Colorado, Illinois, Indiana, Kentucky, Maryland, and Tennessee). Walgreens in 1,500 of their stores (in Oregon, California, New Mexico, Kentucky, Tennessee, Vermont, South Carolina, Illinois, and Indiana). Two of the largest drug stores in the country, and they chose only four of the same states! Yes, there is significant confusion.

Notice, the larger companies are still shying away from any CBD products you ingest. Externally applied CBD seems to be legally interpreted as okay, at least in the states chosen by CVS and Walgreens. Other retailers will not be far behind, as we have expected all along. The nature of competition means others are not going to let the store across the street carry something they don't.

Of the five main ways CBD is being used (lotions and salves, tinctures, infused food and beverage, vape, and pets), we can see topicals being widely accepted first, then tinctures and edibles. Since vaping is a popular delivery method, anyone carrying CBD should consider vape cartridges. Moving CBD products into the mainstream resellers can only help in awareness as well as regulation.

What About Athletes?

If you are an athlete, you are constantly looking to improve performance (notice I did not use the maligned "enhance"). The stress of performing, and the recovery needed after workouts and competition, makes CBD the perfect substance to naturally bring your body back to homeostasis and control inflammation. But, of course, you need to be careful.

Once again, lack of leadership is causing confusion. It seems there are some distinct lines between "performance enhancing" and "mind altering", but still the major associations are inconsistent in interpreting THC and CBD as different. Once again, the fact it is okay to take an opioid for pain, but not a hemp-derived substance, is kind of crazy.

According to Made by Hemp, the World Anti-Doping Agency (WADA) is the first major sports organization to acknowledge CBD as a compound separate from marijuana. As of 2017, CBD is no longer a prohibited substance, as interpreted by WADA. WADA was the first competitive sports association to give their athletes the option to use CBD. Organizations following WADA's guidelines as their own are the International Olympic Committee, International Paralympic Committee, and most of the world's anti-doping organizations.[39]

If the 2020 Olympics had been held (thanks a lot, COVID), it would have been the first Olympics where CBD was considered an allowed substance.[40]

The WADA's threshold for THC is 150 nanograms (ng) per milliliter (ml), which was raised from 15 ng/ml in 2013. 150 ng is the highest threshold of all international leagues. The National Collegiate Athletic Association (NCAA), which regulates the over 1,200 collegiate institutions, conferences, and organizations, has the strictest marijuana testing threshold. Higher than the Federal Aviation Administration

(FAA) and United States military. The THC testing threshold for the NCAA is 5 ng/ml.[41]

CBD is not listed on the NCAA Banned Drugs List, but cannabinoids are; so it is left to the athlete to try to make a case CBD should not be seen as "chemically related" to THC.[42] And, a word of advice, don't do it. There is too much at risk to be the one to try and show the NCAA the benefits of CBD, even if hemp-derived. For lack of direction, you must assume CBD is banned by the NCAA. Scarily, though, there seems to be little pressure to recognize CBD as separate from THC.

The National Football League (NFL) has made strides towards allowing both CBD and THC. For THC, there will no longer be suspensions and the urinary threshold was raised from 35 ng/ml to 150 ng/ml, same as WADA. Plus, the NFLPA is actively reviewing CBD research, and taking it into consideration for chronic pain control.[43] These are major steps for the NFL, one of the more notorious sports for inflammation and injuries. a league where opioids and anti-inflammation drugs are readily prescribed, CBD is still lumped in with THC and banned. You can take OxyContin, but not a leaf. At least in the case of the NFL, there seems to be a groundswell of pressure to change the policy on both CBD and THC. The banned threshold of THC in the NFL is 35 ng/ml. It is thought the new player's agreement will address CBD and THC as necessary for the health of the players.[44]

For the National Basketball Association (NBA), which has also consistently had a harsh stance on THC, the discussion of CBD is at least being reviewed. Both the former Commissioner Stern and current Commissioner Silver have stated medical marijuana should be addressed for the players' health. Unfortunately for the players, though, CBD and THC are still banned substances. Opioids are still okay.... The THC banned level is 15 ng/ml. Progressive disciplinary measures are laid out for violators of the league's banned substance rules. Their next players' agreement is many years off, so the ban will remain in place. It seems like the discussion is there, there are multiple viewpoints, but no action yet.[45]

Major League Baseball (MLB) has a Joint Drug Agreement with the Major League Baseball Players Association (MLBPA), which is lenient towards THC and removed CBD from the banned substances list. This agreement specifically states their intent to focus on "performance enhancing" substances. There is no random drug testing, only for "reasonable cause". If a player exceeds the 50 ng/ml threshold, the player may receive fines- but no suspension.[46]

Strangely enough, there are few outspoken proponents of CBD in the MLB. It must be noted, the MLB's minor league is not under the union agreement of the MLB players, so the minor leagues set their own policies- which are much stricter, and result in suspension and drug treatment.[47]

In the National Hockey League (NHL), the league is mostly focused on "performance enhancing" drugs, so THC and CBD are not banned. They are not encouraged either. In random drug testing, NHL players are tested for cannabinoids, but face no penalties if the substances are found in their system. If positively tested, the league sends that information to their committees to add to the discussion of CBD and THC. If high levels of THC are found in a player, though, that player may be asked to undergo further medical review.[48] Not really sure what that means.

It is hoped the WADA stance on CBD will become more widely accepted, as athletes stand to benefit highly from the natural effects of CBD- and maybe even THC. It's interesting to see the hardline stance by the leagues against CBD, but there is scarcely a mention or two of the horribly addictive effects of opioids and constantly taking anti-inflammatories.

In an interesting juxtaposition that separating CBD from THC may not help in athlete discussion, since most of the talks are about medical marijuana and its benefits.

How is CBD being sourced?

In other developments, and highly encouraging, reviews of how CBD is sourced, processed, and the integrity in the process, has come to the forefront of customers' minds. In our work with resellers, we have found certain best practices being used in choosing the CBD suppliers.

As a consumer, it is suggested you follow the same methods of choosing your products as the stores do- at least until mainstream retailers like Target and Walmart carry all CBD options.

The process to follow:

1. *Review the third-party lab testing.* Is the certifying party accredited, is the product free of contaminants, is the cannabinoid content listed, etc. Are all ingredients listed? Yes, make sure it's third party, and not supported by the company that could benefit (As an aside, did you know all the health benefits claimed by Subway are based upon reviews by "Doctor's Associates", a group of doctors formed by Subway?....always read the fine print).
2. *Does the product contain less than .3% THC?* Yes, you need to check, especially if your employer randomly drug tests. You're usually safe if the hemp source is from one of the industrial hemp farms in the United States (see below). It's best to also do your own internet searches for companies that have had products recalled due to mislabeling. A quick check while writing this book shows Kore Organic CBD being recalled due to lead, the FDA finding half of the CBD products tested containing THC, , and another test by the FDA where only 45% of the product tested contained CBD within 20% of what was stated on the label! [49] [50] [51]
3. *What is the hemp source and cultivation method?* United States hemp is best, and there are some specific hemp farms in Colorado, North Carolina, and Kentucky. Make

sure it is U.S. hemp! Nothing against China, but you are trusting your health and your drug tests to a foreign grower and a product with no FDA specifications yet! The FDA has been so focused on those making health claims, they still have not developed criteria for product quality. They are both important, granted, but people are already buying the product.

4. *What is the type of CBD used?* Is it labeled Isolate, Full Spectrum, or Broad Spectrum? Full Spectrum is your best bet, based upon the entourage effect of the other cannabinoids. Isolate, though, may be used if you experience stomach issues from CBD, or absolutely do not want any trace of THC in the product- as long as it's labeled correctly.

5. *How is it extracted?* CO_2 extraction is standard, where pressurized carbon dioxide preserves the terpenes. One of the more reputable companies, Sunsoil, uses organic hemp grown on its own farm and extracts the CBD oil with heat and a lipid (either MCT oil or coconut oil).[52] MCT oil tends to work well with the body's system to increase bioavailability.

6. *How much CBD is in each dose?* This is surprisingly quite confusing for CBD products. Issues range from needing 25 CBD gummy bears for any impact to not really understanding what a label might mean when it states "10 mg CBD per serving, 600 mg total CBD, serving size 1 ml" when you are taking it in a dropper (tincture).

7. *Is it a fair price, for the dosage?* Once again, the amount of CBD in each product will reflect the potency. When you vary by potency, but the product looks the same, it can be confusing. If the same bottle of CBD has either 600 mg total or 1,200 mg total, and the bottle looks the same- the consumer is confused when the 1,200 mg is twice the price. As with most products, value is in the eye of the consumer, as long as they can trust you are labeling properly. Most CBD manufacturers show very little pricing creativity. If it's double the milligrams, it's double the price.

8. *What is the reputation of the producer?* Yes, websites are the first place to look, although a company's own website

is probably not going to point you to any issues about their own company. Why would they? Find third party sites like CBD Origin or Leafly.
9. *Is this product legal in your state?* Simple, right? Legality has been so clearly interpreted by each state. What's so hard about this step? ☺

The Case for Cannabis

If you do not know we have an opioid crisis in this country, and this world, you are not paying attention. It's bad. Really bad. Don't take it from me, as I am not an opioid expert. Cooper Smith, speaking for the Addiction Center states, "The opioid epidemic specifically refers to the growing number of deaths and hospitalizations from opioids, including prescriptions, illicit drugs, and analogues. In recent years, death rates from these drugs have ramped up to over 40,000 a year, or 115 a day, across the United States. Drug overdose is now the leading cause of accidental death in the United States, largely due to the opioid epidemic. The opioid epidemic first gained notoriety around 2010, but the factors behind it had begun several years earlier."[53]

Opioids are a classification of drug that is derived from, or a synthetic version of, opium. Morphine was used for years as a pain reliever. Some opioids, like methadone, were developed due to a scarcity of morphine, while others, like heroin, were made in an attempt to make less addictive drugs. "Today, opioids are almost synonymous with pain relief."[54]

Examples of common opioids include codeine, Demerol, fentanyl, hydrocodone, and oxycodone. If you own stock in Purdue Pharma, makers of OxyContin, or are friends with the Sackler family, or have accepted money from the Sackler family, you are clearly feeling the heat right now as lawsuits are piling up accusing the company and its founding Sackler family of aggressively pushing this drug on doctors for their patients- while knowing the addictive dangers.[55]

According to Smith, "As pharmaceutical companies were looking for new pain killers, they began to push synthetic and semi-synthetic opioids to doctors. The companies would say the drugs were either less- or non-addictive in comparison to morphine, and had no dangerous side effects. Naturally, doctors began pushing these drugs as they saw no repercussions to patients taking them. This growth in the prescription opioid business directly pushed the distribution of opioids to levels that remain to this day, contributing to the epidemic we are now dealing with."[56]

Staggeringly, we lose 115 people a day, on average, to opiate deaths. Even more incredibly, 80% of people suffering from an addiction to heroin started with a prescription for an opioid pain reliever. It is only after their prescription ends that many users realize they've become dependent upon the effects of opioids to function "normally."

At that point, they are either forced to quit using opioids, and endure the pain that comes with the withdrawal, or look for other means of getting their high. This is often the time where people will turn to illicit drugs or other analogues. Heroin is often cheaper, more potent, and easier to locate than what they were taking before. In fact, about 80% of people using heroin started with a prescription to another opioid. After using heroin, however, 23% of individuals develop opioid addiction.[57]

The number of people dying of accidental overdose of opioids eclipses every other drug combined, which is why the term "opioid epidemic" was coined. In 2015, the US saw 52,404 deaths from drug overdose. More than 20,000 of those were from prescription pain relievers, and close to 13,000 were from heroin. That means 63% of drug deaths were tied to opioids. That number of opioid-related deaths grew by nearly 10,000 the following year.

The scary part is these are not people who are using heroin or some other illegal drug. These are people who are using medication they got from a doctor. In 1992, before the major push for opioids from pharmaceutical companies, doctors wrote 112 million opioid prescriptions. In 2016, the number of opioid prescriptions had increased to 236 million after a peak of 282 million in 2014.[58]

Houston, we have a problem. Our trusted medical professionals are able to prescribe one of the most addictive substances known to man to a 14 year old, knowing that kid may never be able to get off those drugs. Anyone supporting opioids and pushing off CBD research should be forced to go to addiction centers, hospitals, and morgues to see what opioids have done to our population!

But, why opioids?

The underlying issue of opioid use comes from something being "wrong" with our body. We've either had an accident, and need to control the pain; or, we have chronic inflammation, and need to control the pain. Or, we have treatments for other illnesses, and need to control the pain. You get the point. Our bodies get out of whack. Sometimes temporarily, sometimes long term. It is not surprising we would seek out ways to either cover our pain or even control the source of the pain. It's also not surprising we would want the feeling back when we run out of the drugs.

But, what if there were a natural way to impact our bodies positively, in regards to pain and its underlying causes? There is a substance that could help our bodies, it is a natural substance, and has no overdose ability? In fact, even the addictive properties are inconclusive. That's what we have in hemp-derived CBD!

In my first CBD book, *CBD Dreams*, we described the Endocannabinoid System (ECS). This system is a self-regulating system containing receptors throughout our bodies. These receptors work together as a lock and key. When the ECS system is working properly, our bodies produce our own phytocompounds, called endocannabinoids. These compounds help the ECS in its job to communicate with every system in our body, including all our organs, the Central Nervous System, our Immune System, etc.[59]

The primary function of the ECS is to promote homeostasis, or the "self-regulating process by which biological systems tend to maintain stability while adjusting to conditions that are optimal for survival. If homeostasis is successful, life continues; if unsuccessful, disaster or death ensues. The stability attained is actually a dynamic equilibrium, in which continuous change occurs yet relatively uniform conditions prevail."[60]

We didn't know about our body's reaction to CBD (or THC) until as recently as 1988. More specifically, we didn't know about how cannabis and THC interacted with our ECS. In the 60's, it's probably not clear how anything interacted with anything, except it was a "high" that was sought after by a large portion of the population. As with everything, scientists are always looking for connections![61]

According to CBD Origins, a team of researchers discovered a cannabinoid receptor in rats that interacted exclusively with receptors found in the cannabis compound, Tetrahydrocannabinol (THC). Even cooler, the receptors were found concentrated in parts of the brain responsible for mental and physiological processes, like memory, high cognition, emotion, and motor coordination.[62]

When a second cannabinoid receptor was identified in rats that was distributed throughout the immune system and peripheral tissues of the body, and had the same reaction to THC as the first receptor, then a larger picture began to form. The clues led scientists to search for these receptors in other beings. And, yes, you guessed it- they found them in humans. They called these receptors CB1 and CB2.[63]

Now bear with me, this is where it gets a little confusing: researchers were able to further analyze the relationship between the cannabinoid receptors within our body (endocannabinoids) and the cannabinoid receptors in cannabis compounds like CBD and THC (both called phytocannabinoids). What was found was a previously unknown signaling system between phytocannabinoids and endocannabinoids. Our bodies were designed to engage with cannabinoids. These discoveries were the origin of the Endocannabinoid System.[64] And since that time, further research has uncovered additional cannabinoids with specific health benefits to our bodies. These cannabinoids, like CBN, CBG, and THCV were discussed earlier and affirm the need to consider the entire plant when discussing cannabis.

A Research Review

Cannabidiol (CBD) sales are projected to continue rising at a rapid rate for years, as stigma abates and awareness increases. According to a study by the *Hemp Business Journal*, consumer sales of CBD are set to equal 5 billion dollars in the next few years, which would be a staggering increase from the $108.1 million sales in 2014.[65]

In terms of competition, a few firms are battling for market share of the CBD industry in the United States. Many companies, such as Canopy Growth, have undertaken massive research and development campaigns in order to grab as much CBD market share as possible. According to a *Pot Network* article, Canopy Growth has acquired research assets from outside companies and is poised to "stay competitive on this side of the cannabis industry".[66] Tilray, a Canadian pharmaceutical company, is making moves into the United States market as well. Their largest move to date is signing with Authentic Brand Group, who owns such subsidiaries as Nine West and Juicy Couture. Their plan is to use this agreement as an inroad to what Kuhl describes as "leverage their portfolio in order to develop, market and distribute a brand of consumer cannabis products, including CBD".[67] Have you noticed the price of hothouse tomatoes skyrocketing? It's because those greenhouses can yield higher dollars when used for hemp. Sorry, lycopene, you're just not cool anymore.

The Farm Bill of 2018 significantly put CBD on the map, along with the wave of legalization of THC. The Farm Bill is an informal term for a body of legislation that covers broad agricultural and food policy, and is typically amended and voted on every five years. It does not normally cover cannabis, but it was brought to the forefront of the conversation by Senate Majority Leader Mitch McConnell, who advocated strongly for hemp's legalization. According to the Brookings Institute, McConnell's push involved legalizing hemp, which is the portion of cannabis that "cannot contain more than 0.3% of THC".[68] This move was eventually included in the final version of the bill that was ultimately signed by President Trump at the end of 2018.

Prior to this move by McConnell and the Republican Congress, CBD was almost completely illegal, as it was classified by the Controlled Substances Act as a Schedule 1 drug. According to the US Drug Enforcement Administration (DEA), Schedule 1 drugs are classified as drugs "with no currently accepted medical use and a high potential for abuse".[69]

Examining a summary report on CBD oil put out by the Brightfield Group, this report aimed to establish a baseline for CBD users based off the 2,400 respondents who were members of the HelloMD medicinal cannabis community. Brightfield's report offered a well-derived summation that diagrammed uses, ingestion methods, as well as current manufacturing brands. Interestingly, this study revealed that, of its respondents, 58% of CBD "only" users were women.[70] While this study does offer insight, it falls short in that its chosen respondents are sourced from an online cannabis community.

A possible reason for a lack of awareness regarding CBD is public distrust. In an article published to *Science Direct*, Nancy Shute advises readers to pump the brakes regarding CBD and its purported far-reaching relief. Shute states that "the science is skimpy at best", and that people looking into CBD use often encounter "a muddle of marketing masquerading as impartial information".[71]

Continuing the literature review, nearly all available sources seemed to draw a direct correlation between CBD and THC, as we've alluded to repeatedly in this book. For example, a report from the *Pharmacology and Therapeutics Journal* has positive words for CBD while comparing it directly to THC, stating it "is undoubtedly the more interesting cannabinoid with a lot of reported pharmacological effects in several models of pathologies, ranging from inflammatory and neurodegenerative diseases, to epilepsy, autoimmune disorders like multiple sclerosis, arthritis, schizophrenia and cancer."[72]

While some studies did delineate a difference between CBD and THC, none aimed at individual substance awareness. Another common theme found in available CBD research was tied to a specific ailment and the redeeming qualities of CBD. While this information is useful, it still did not gauge an individual respondent's overall awareness level.

The extent to which consumers are educated about CBD's properties varies. CBD is gaining publicity from the endorsement of some professional athletes, including UFC fighters Yair Rodriguez and Nate Diaz, ultramarathon runner Avery Collins, and Tennessee Titans linebacker Derrick Morgan. All have come out and stated they use CBD to help with recovery, sore muscles, and achy joints- and also to combat general inflammation.[73]

Athletes are not the only credible sources for CBD pain relief, however. Some healthcare practitioners are seemingly prescribing the product with praise, as 90% of them who prescribed CBD explained "the technology provides more effective pain relief for their patients than over-the-counter analgesics.[74] Roughly 40% of U.S. adults age 21 and over indicated a willingness to explore CBD under the right conditions, according to a study by High Yield Insights. The study found the majority of those interested are 35 years or older, female, and have college experience.[75]

The majority of the peer reviewed research has been performed on cannabinoids and their impact on the pain control of patients suffering from debilitating illnesses. According to Campbell et al, "humans have cannabinoid receptors in the central and peripheral nervous system in animal testing cannabinoids are analgesic and reduce signs of neuropathic pain. Some evidence exists that cannabinoids may be analgesic in humans.[76]

In other research, it was found short-term use of existing medical cannabinoids appeared to increase the risk of non-serious adverse events. The risks associated with long-term use were poorly characterized in published clinical trials and observational studies. High-quality trials of long-term exposure are required to further characterize safety issues related to the use of medical cannabinoids.[77]

Researchers have been investigating the anti-cancer properties held within CBD, along with other medical related issues. Research is currently being conducted on the benefits of CBD, where potential claims to treating a wide range of problems like "arthritis, diabetes, alcoholism, MS, chronic pain, PTSD, depression, antibiotic- resistant infections are being found".[78] Many people fail to realize that most commercial CBD is actually derived from hemp, which has little to no THC.[79] Research and evidence has the chance to influence the perception of individuals, thus affecting how those around them view CBD.[80]

Prior to legalization, not many people knew there were health benefits related to CBD and believed it gave people the same high as marijuana, which is false. This article discusses the many different topical treatments CBD can offer, as well as all the different skin issues it can treat.[81]

Another article discusses the main differences between cannabidiol and marijuana. It discusses how CBD is used to treat a wide variety of health issues, mainly childhood epilepsy syndromes. CBD is also known for providing relief for those with anxiety, insomnia, and those who cannot stay asleep. It is stressed that while many components about CBD are known, one thing that is not known is the most therapeutic dose of CBD for any specific medical condition.[82]

An additional article addresses more in-depth how beneficial CBD can be to the skin. Because CBD has been shown to help with inflammation, and acne is a by-product of inflammation, CBD can be effective in healing acne and providing relief for many other skin issues. Because CBD is an antibacterial and anti-inflammatory, it helps to dissolve oil and other bacteria that can be trapped in the skin. This study also shows that whether one is taking CBD orally or applying it topically, both methods proved successful in achieving better skin in most participants.[83]

Additional articles discuss the differential effectiveness of selected non-psychotropic phytocannabinoids on human sebocyte functions, and their introduction in dry/ seborrhoeic skin and acne treatment. This article explores the effect of cannabinoids on the skin and how it can help with acne (differential effectiveness of selected non-psychotropic phytocannabinoids on human sebocyte functions implicates their introduction in dry/ seborrhoeic skin and acne treatment).[84]

Further research discusses treatment with cannabis and cannabinoids: some practical aspects and controversies, particularly for patients with chronic conditions, oral administration could be a big advantage because it doesn't require frequent dosing throughout the day.[85]

Additional research discusses CBD skin care market insights: growth factors, market drivers, segmentations, key players, analysis and forecast by 2027. It reviews the CBD skin care sales and the demand growth of CBD products specifically related to skin.[86]

Companies advertising pet treats are claiming they can help pets with anxiety, arthritis, and cancer. Along with treating those symptoms, people are giving CBD to their pets to help with separation anxiety and noise phobia. Many pet owners report positive outcomes after giving pets CBD. There is a lack of FDA approval, and no clinical studies for animals have been done to prove these claims. Even with the lack of approval and studies, the CBD for pet market is booming.[87]

In Colorado, an anonymous survey was given to pet owners who buy CBD products from an online company. The survey returned 632 responses, where 58.8% of respondents claimed they use a hemp product for their dogs. They found 93% felt the CBD treats performed equally or better than other medicines. Pet owners noticeably see these treats as performing the same or equally than other medicines, and only 7% reported that CBD does not perform as well.[88]

Since CBD use with pets is fairly new, there is little research available about the use of it and the long and short term effects are still unknown. This means veterinarians are not able to determine safe doses of CBD for pets. The American Veterinary Medical Association (AVMA) is urging vets to make treatment decisions based upon clinical judgment, current medical information that is available, and make sure they comply with the current laws and regulations. Currently, most vets are suggesting pet owners use caution when giving their animals CBD products.[89]

In order to gain more information on CBD for pets, we reviewed some select websites that sell pet treats. The first website was for the company Honest Paws. On their website, there is a dosage calculator where you input information about your pet, their birthday, weight, what kind, and what symptoms your pet has that you are trying to treat. They then give their suggestions on what kind of CBD you should get for your pet based upon this information. It is important for these companies to have a section explaining CBD, so anyone visiting it can be informed.[90]

Pet Releaf, which had a similar layout as Honest Paws, also has a usage calculator to help customers find the best product for their pets. There are multiple options and ways of giving your pet CBD. This calculator makes it easier for customers to narrow it down and pick from a few options. They also have a Frequently Asked Questions sections, where they answer the most popular questions asked like what is CBD, is it safe, is it legal, and many more. These websites created sections of their page just to explain what CBD is, so customers do not have to do their own research.[91]

CBD could balloon into a 22 billion dollar industry, but with so many laws being changed there are only a few regulation or packaging requirements.[92] Companies like Cannabinoid Creations are already creating foods, snacks, and sparkling drinks all infused with CBD.[93] According to a report from the World Health Organization, "CBD exhibits no effects indicative of any abuse or dependence up to date, there is no evidence of public health related problems associated with the use of pure CBD".[94]

Although the federal government legalized CBD that is derived from hemp, the FDA's rules still prohibit companies and restaurants from adding it to food or drinks.[95] The list of states where medical or recreational use of marijuana and CBD is legal, keeps growing. CBD products sold online run the gamut, from tinctures and creams, to gummies and pills, to coffees and teas. CBD products are often marketed as anti-inflammatories and pain relievers that can also help with insomnia and anxiety.[96] Between THC and CBD, there is significant overlap and a ripeness for confusion.

With its reported benefits, CBD has become an increasingly popular additive in consumer products. It has shown up in topical oils, skin creams, food, and drinks.[97] Comparing it to the feeling after an intense meditation or yoga session, one author added the CBD glow has "synergistic downstream effects" in terms of social connections. A detox drink under development called Sober Up, for example, will contain CBD and is supposed to support liver health and help prevent hangovers.[98] As stated above, CBD infused foods are becoming more prevalent in society as CBD is becoming legalized. CBD and THC are a large cookie jar right now, with multiple hands reaching in for a cookie. The educated consumer does his or her own research, stays up to date on trends, and is overtly curious about the topic.

What are the benefits of THC/CBD?

It starts and ends with homeostasis. What was found is that endocannabinoids are present throughout a large majority of the functions of the body, and help maintain proper functioning of our ECS. Through aging, or any of the other things in life that impact our bodies, our body's parts and systems deteriorate and malfunction. When this happens, it affects the entire body and can lead to various health problems.[99]

Endocannabinoids can only do so much, once the body begins to deteriorate. What the body needs are phytocannabinoids (like CBD) to help bring health levels up in the body. As we discussed, the ECS has two main receptors, CB1 and CB2. THC bonds with both receptors, and CBD only bonds with the CB2 receptor- the main reason THC gives you the "high". When CBD bonds with the CB2 receptors, it has been shown to improve the capabilities of that receptor, and thus improving functionality of the receptors. Plus, if the body is experiencing a cannabinoid deficiency, CBD can close the gap. A cannabinoid deficiency can result in inflammation, headaches, etc.[100]

When you ingest CBD, and it bonds with our CB2 receptors, it helps in the maintenance of health functions; plus it helps in the restoration of homeostasis. If the out of balance body is the cause of many of our health issues, CBD is here to help us regain our balance. There are three main areas that have been shown to benefit from CBD:

Inflammation- One of the main issues impacting all of us is inflammation. According to medical professionals, "inflammation is part of the body's immune response. It can be beneficial when, for example, your knee sustains a blow and tissues need care and protection. However, sometimes, inflammation can persist longer than necessary, causing more harm than benefit."[101]   CBD attacks inflammation by suppressing inflammatory response and pathways, stimulating the production of regulatory cells, and managing our pain perception.[102]

Seizures- Seizures are usually more disease-specific, and are caused by erratic electrical activity in the brain, causing the body to shake violently. CBD has proven to greatly reduce seizures in patients suffering from Dravet Syndrome and Lennox-Gaustat Syndrome, two severe forms of epilepsy. According to *CBD Origin*, CBD reduces seizures by slowing down excitatory nerve activity and subduing the brain's reaction to the intensified signals that cause the brain to overload.[103]

Stress and Anxiety- Stress and anxiety often occur due to your response to a dangerous or undesirable situation. An imbalance of hormones or excessive messages within the brain will increase your cortisol levels, causing you to feel stressed. CBD combats stress by regulating how your brain responds to stress signals and maintaining your cortisol levels.[104] Relieving stress also aid in helping our bodies go to sleep. So, as a byproduct, CBD also helps us sleep.

According to one leading retailer in the space, "CBD is known to aid in stress, anxiety, nausea, and other ailments. People are also using it to naturally treat chronic pain, sleep deprivation and a variety of other ailments, including extreme conditions such as Epilepsy and Alzheimer's. CBD interacts with our naturally occurring systems and doesn't cause a high, making it a safer, less controversial wellness alternative, while still offering significant health benefits."[105]

Keep in mind, the three areas above, when out of whack, impact our sleep. The one great solution to our health issues could be sleep. And, as we're about to find out, it's exactly what many customers are saying. Let's dive into the uses and benefits a bit further, ranked by effectiveness, as gauged by customer and consumer comments.

What do the people say?

Probably the number one issue being identified as helped by CBD is sleep. The difficulty in identifying and claiming benefits of anything would be entourage impacts, or even upstream and downstream variables. If you are using something for inflammation, and that substance helps you sleep at night, which then lowers your inflammation levels, did it help sleep or inflammation? See how medical researchers have a such a difficult time being able to draw causal relationships. They can find associations, but may not be able to find causations.

But, I will tell you from my research, as well as my own interviews (and personal experience), sleep deprivation is bubbling up to be the number one issue being affected positively by CBD. My personal experience, I had not slept a full night for years. Years! If I take as little as 15mg of CBD before bed, I sleep like a baby. The number of testimonials around CBD and sleep are too numerous to ignore. Call it anecdotal, call it hearsay, it doesn't matter. If you cannot sleep a full night, you are in trouble. If you're not convinced, check out the *Ted Talk* by Matt Walker titled "Sleep is your superpower".[106]

Chronic pain, normally also referred to as chronic inflammation, is another one of the top issues identified by CBD users as why they are partaking of CBD products. As described in the ECS description, CBD can help repair and restore cells, as well as control or inhibit pain.

Closely ranked with inflammation is using CBD for overall calmness. This one seems like the scariest to those still defining CBD and THC synonymously as the same substance (seriously, if you're still doing that, it's your own ignorance....you're not listening!). A sense of calm, relieving anxiety, helping you sort out your thoughts, and helping with awareness, are all touted as results from CBD products.

All the issues listed above are real, and the other link? They all have synthetic drugs available to address the issue, readily prescribed by medical professionals. Legally prescribed!

Which forms are preferred?

In the discussion of how cannabinoids are introduced into the body, we can think in term of all cannabinoids being the same. THC and CBD, and the rest, can all be introduced to the body in the same ways- including a few new ones we'll cover you'll want to sit down for! If you noticed in the research review, the forms of CBD are starting to be sorted as either preferred, or seen as being more like a placebo. In this section, we'll look at the forms and what the customers are pointing out are the advantages and disadvantages of each form. The forms we will cover are topicals and lotions, tinctures or drops, infused food and beverage grocery stores, infused food and beverage consumed away from home, vaping, pre-rolls/bongs, and pets.

Topicals and lotions

Inside this category, we will also include bath oils, roll-ons, etc. Any method of applying CBD to the outside of the body, and not ingesting the product, is in this category. If you ask customers, applying THC/CBD externally is trending as highly effective and useful. The usefulness comes from the portability of the packages, the various sizes, and the multiple uses. Applying CBD to sore muscles and using in massages is becoming popular. Hosting CBD massage parties is rocking! Thank the Kardashians for that one.

Among the best-selling new products of the last 12 months, at least 50% of them involve applying CBD externally. Body creams tend to be enhanced with botanicals like juniper, lavender, eucalyptus, and lemongrass (paralleling the trend in vodka and gin), and are available in both CBD and THC. Sleeping masks and bath bombs round out topicals.

It must be noted topicals take roughly fifteen to thirty minutes to work on your body, and the effect lasts four to five hours (depending upon mg applied, of course).

Tinctures or drops

These varieties have suffered a bit. In fact, the majority of the customers we asked are quite confused by tinctures. It doesn't feel "normal" to lift your tongue and apply drops under it (sublingually). It is also exceedingly difficult to understand doses, milligrams per dose, and why it costs so much. Tinctures have suffered because it is quite the cash outlay to try something that costs $35 to $70, with some running $200. That's not the definition of an impulse purchase.

In fact, a large percentage of customers use drops to add to their food or drink on their own. From their comments, and similarly to cooking on your own, customers know how much is going in their food or beverage, and they feel pretty good about having that control. Tinctures have a lot of work to do in terms of educating the customers about potency levels and costs associated with the purity of what is offered in the bottles.

For timing of effect, tinctures delivered properly (under your tongue, sublingually) will take effect almost immediately, and have the most impact if using proper dosage and milligrams. If you add it to your food or beverage, CBD delivered by tincture must work through your digestion system and will take roughly forty-five minutes to impact your body. If you are looking for immediate impact of any cannabinoid, you must avoid the digestion system.

Infused food and beverage consumed at home

Like consuming alcohol at the bar or restaurant versus buying it to consume at home, customers report various preferences for both methods of consumption. For buying food and beverage at the store, gummy bears are still the preferred method of delivering THC/CBD into the digestive system, with chocolate and brownies about to catch up and pass those little gummies. Gummy bears, for some strange reason, are preferred almost four to one as the delivery method to the body.

Coming in second in infused food is the candy bar. It seems like snacks take the cake (so to speak) in CBD delivery. As for beverages, you have water for already infused and ready to drink beverages, and you have tea and coffee for something that must be prepared before consumption. Alcohol is a tricky one. Alcohol is having a difficult time being accepted as a delivery mechanism for THC/ CBD. Most consumers state it's the concern about mixing alcohol and cannabinoids. Many are still leery about whether or not CBD will "get them high", and mixing with alcohol, at least purchased at the store, has not caught on in popularity. When you do go to pick up that THC or CBD beer, take a look at the alcohol content. The abv is pretty much at a non-alcohol level. It just tastes like beer.

I am going to include capsules in the infused food section of this book, primarily because you are introducing CBD into the digestive system. If there is a trend set to take off, it's capsules of CBD. They are pre-measured (easy to understand what to take), easy to transport, and can be hidden amongst your other medications (if you still take them). Remember, consumers are also looking to not look like junkies, and hiding their ingestion of CBD is still top of mind.

Infused food and beverage away from home

This trend is rocking! Hosting CBD food parties, offering CBD smoothies, CBD infused kombucha, etc. These areas are on fire. Think of it this way, anything that has been seen as healthy is now seen as healthier and trendier when you add CBD to it.

Even alcohol, where legal (or served and hoping no one catches them), is trendy when you add CBD to it. The big issue of CBD consumed on premise is not quite knowing if the restaurant or bar did the appropriate homework to ensure they are not giving you THC, or are only giving you top quality products from reliable sources. Just like serving crappy fish (like tilapia), running restaurants is a balance between serving customers cool stuff and finding the cheapest ingredients possible. I would strongly suggest you keep as much control of your CBD as possible, which means either go to a restaurant or bar where you know they are doing the right thing for the customer, or do it yourself at home.

Vaping

Anything to do with vaping carries with it the stigma of all other types of smoking. If you want the CBD to hit you instantly, vaping is the way to go. If you want people to stare at you like you're a loser, vaping is the way to go….the stigma is off the charts for vaping. The trends show vaping is wildly more popular with those who are looking to inhale THC. It fits the mold, and anyone looking to inhale THC is not too worried about what you think- especially in a state like California where it is widely accepted and is widespread. I was in San Diego recently and I think I got high just walking down the sidewalk!

If you're okay vaping in public, then go for it. The CBD will hit you immediately, and everything will be okay!

Pre-rolls and Bongs

If vaping has stigma, pre-rolls and bongs have stigma x 1,000! This method of intaking THC is as close to Cheech and Chong and Snoop Dogg as you can get. Pre-rolls are exactly as you would expect. You do not need to roll your own, can be inexpensive, and come with quite the dank smell! And bongs are even more "hard core", in regards to the process of heating the dried flower in a bowl and water inserted into the bong. Once lit, the smoke is drawn through the water and the user (might as well say stoner, at this point) inhales from the bong so bubbles containing smoke come from the stem.

It's like a matcha tea ceremony, but different. This delivery method is almost completely for THC, with very few people using pre-rolls for CBD.

Pet CBD

Addressing pet CBD is important for two reasons: pets have issues with bones, and pet owners are already giving human CBD to their pets. This is the one instance where CBD is highly preferred by pet owners over THC. As you can imagine, pet treats are the most popular delivery mechanism for pet CBD. If a pet refuses a treat, you have bigger issues than bones! The next preferred method is tinctures dropped on the food. In this case, you might as well get the animal a treat. You are over-spending and then delivering it to your pet in the same manner as a treat.

We are talking primarily dogs here, with cats a distant second. Dogs have so many fear issues and bone issues, pet CBD usage for dogs is off the charts! Dogs are kind of scaredy cats, and seem to have the worst built hips of all animals.

The second reason to talk about pet CBD is many humans are giving pets human dosages. This is a big mistake! Pets react differently to CBD, and dosages must be adhered to militantly. Giving a dog a human dosage of CBD will clearly take care of any jumpiness your dog used to have- they'll be bombed out of their minds and sitting in the corner drooling. Don't do it!

What will make CBD accepted?

The people who produce CBD products, and then use some kind of juiced-up "get you high" messaging in their branding and labeling, are not helping themselves. They're not helping anyone! They are basically feeding into the lack of knowledge and using it to their advantage. And, as a whole, they are hurting an industry that can actually help people. Neon green, fluorescent, all that kind of romanticizing of "getting high" needs to be eliminated! It is keeping the major national consumer goods companies away from hemp-derived CBD. Plus, they're scaring off retailers.

So, back to the question, is it accepted? Notice I did not say "acceptable". I specifically mean "accepted". Is it okay to carry something labeled CBD (hemp-derived) with you to school, to church, to a friend's house? Well, you'll have to answer that one yourself. If you feel uncomfortable, then avoid it. No one is forcing you to consume anything. On the other hand, it's not something to be ashamed of, and certainly is not something that has been shown to be harmful. In fact, if you have read the material on the product, know what you are doing, and want to consume it, then it might be a great way to spread the word about the benefits, if you so desire.

Think about it this way, if you like the product, and more companies become engaged in the production and selling of it, then the worst thing that can happen is your price will come down. Is that so bad? It's kind of expensive, so there is room for a price leveling to take effect.

If you've decided to try it, one area I'm not going to cover in this book is how much should you take. We all vary in weight, height, tolerance for anything, etc. The best suggestion is to start small and work up until you feel an impact. You know, if it gets you off anti-depressants, then you win, right? Those things are as addictive as heroin.

Where do you go from here?

There is a compelling case that THC and CBD and the assorted cannabinoids being discovered in the cannabis plant, can be life-changing for some and helpful to many. If this information provided gets one person off synthetic pain pills, then there's a victory. In my opinion, one victory is enough. Many victories would be a cherry on top.

You've got to make your own decisions about what you ingest or apply or vape or whatever. The previous pages have contained up to date information from research, from interviews, from social media sites, from retailers, etc. Almost every bit of information is pointing to THC/CBD being substances that can help us get off the opioid addictions, the synthetic drug usage, and the endless cycle of fighting inflammation.

If you ask me, I'd say yes, you need to try it. This book has reflected a personal journey of mine to educate the public to the best of my ability. I believe strongly in the benefits from the cannabis plant, especially when it could possibly disconnect us from the tentacles of big pharma and its influence on our medical professionals. Just remember, you don't have to get high to enjoy the benefits; and if you do want to get high, that's a personal decision you're allowed to make.

Good luck!

This next section is for retailers and consumer packaged goods companies.

Sure, it's legal, but should I carry it in my store?

Okay, so here's where we'll switch gears a little and focus on food retailers. I've spent my entire life in food retail, before I began teaching it, and happen to think this industry is a trendsetter in most countries. People look to our stores for guidance, they trust we are looking out for them, and they want us to provide information that can help them in their lives. When you consider all of the above, the hemp-derived CBD category is screaming for food retailers to grab it and go! And, if you want to get into the THC business, it's right there waiting for you.

Should you carry it? I've laid out an argument that suggests you should carry hemp-derived CBD products. You might still be wondering, similar to the above personal argument, about whether you will be judged harshly by critics, whether you'll be held up as an example of why the world is going to hell in a hand basket, and you're worried. First suggestion, stop worrying. It's a legal product. Your job is to be on top of trends and be there before the customers. I'd say if you're just now thinking about it, you're not doing your job. You should already have a plan as to how you can offer this legal product to your customers. And, guess what, they're wondering what is taking you so long. If you're thinking of getting into THC, then you're at least progressive enough to see a trend that might need to be addressed. *One word of warning for CBD-only retailers: when THC comes to town legally, selling only CBD is not going to cut it. THC wins when CBD and THC compete.*

Second, get off your high horse if you think there is a stigma attached to it. If you're so concerned about critics, and so concerned about your customers, then here's the list of items to pull out of your stores right now:

- Atlantic salmon is over-fished and under-exercised. It's actually bad for you!
- Red and yellow dyes are actually bad for you. You heard me M&M's. Love you guys, but that stuff kills.
- High fructose corn syrup is still widely and happily available in so many products! It is horrible for you, but hey Coke sells, doesn't it?
- Sugar, sugar, sugar, sugar, sugar, sugar....it's everywhere and causes a ton of inflammation- which can be controlled by....CBD....think of it as a virtuous loop.
- The entire processed deli meat section.
- Coffee creamer sections. The whole section is a trans-fat factory.
- And you still sell cigarettes?

Okay, maybe you get my point. The customers are looking to you to help them understand. When people don't understand, they get confused and angry, and then they see those fluorescent green labels making it look like you'll get high, and there you have it. No knowledge means people make stuff up!

As you might imagine, I think you should be all over this category as a retailer!

Okay, I'll carry it, now what?

According to Rick Maturo, from Nielsen (quoted in *Supermarket News*), "For supermarkets and other food retailers, CBD really is a pretty attractive consideration. Number one, it definitely has the ability to drive new customers to the store, so you can steal share from competitors and get more brands to come into the store. It also has the ability to increase the basket for existing customers. So someone coming into your store and spending 'X' number of dollars could be spending $30 or $40 more if you're stocking some of these CBD products."[107]

I'd strongly suggest you take this category through the category management process. It's the only way to wrap your head around what it is, what it isn't, how to communicate it, how to shelve it, etc. Let's do that together. Following the steps from Category Management Principles, here's probably the best way to understand a category that is too trendy to ignore, but is full of uncertainty and mis-information.[108]

As a retailer, there are some key steps to take to ensure your credibility is maintained in the eyes of CBD consumers:

1. **Treat CBD like a category.** Run it through a category plan, designate sub-categories, integrate yourself into the minds of the consumer, and actively understand the inventory flow to maintain in-stock conditions.
2. **Stay on trend.** It's an explosive category, with almost unlimited upward potential. You need to stay on trend and up to date on legislation, rules, new cannabinoids, sub-categories, etc.
3. **Have an expert in house.** There needs to be a "go to" expert on all things CBD. It's the only way to ensure you

have a view inside the consumer's head. Preferably, this person should be a consumer of CBD.

4. **Active and passive selling.** The expert is your active seller, but that person is not always available. Like wine, consumers want information. Passive point of sale material goes a long way towards establishing credibility. As a side note, the lockboxes are not only theft deterrents, but are also sales deterrents. Yes, CBD is expensive, but it's a pretty quick turnoff when a customer needs to find someone with a key.

5. **Protect your customers.** Run your own quality assurance, ensure the product is USDA Organic, etc. Organic is our best solution to ensure the product at least meets some standards. Plus, hemp is a ground "vacuum cleaner", sucking up everything around it. If it's not organic, you have no idea how many pesticides, heavy metals, etc. are in the product. And please make sure you vet any CBD biomass or products not being grown in the United States.

6. **Stay informed.** Similar to #2, become an expert on all things CBD. Read Leafly, WebMD, CBD Daily, etc. to see what's happening in the marketplace.

7. **Weed out suppliers.** In this case, a wide assortment of suppliers will probably hurt you. Choose a few, get to know them and their processes. You'll be better off in the long run.

8. **Whole health solution.** If you are a food store, you are still the only store available that can offer organic produce, self-care solutions, even a pharmacy. Play yourself up as a whole health solution. CBD users are highly informed consumers and will appreciate the fact you are attempting to offer a lifestyle solution for them and their families.

Two definitions to keep in mind:

Category- Distinct, manageable group of products/services that consumers perceive to be interrelated and/or substitutable in meeting a consumer need.

Category Management- Retailer/Supplier process of managing categories as strategic business units, producing enhanced business results by focusing on delivering consumer value.[109]

Hemp-Derived Cannabidiol Category Plan

Introduction / Opportunity

Through environmental scanning, it is apparent that CBD and CBD-infused products are emerging as a trend. The fact that marijuana is seeing a push for legalization, is potentially driving awareness of CBD and its potential benefits. Customers are confused as to what is legal, what is CBD, will it get you high, etc. Undeniably, though, all predictions point to the CBD marketplace exploding in the next few years, with predictions of total market sales to be anywhere between $2B to $20B within five years.[110] Clearly there is uncertainty, but as a consumer goods company or as a food retailer, these opportunities present themselves infrequently and must be pursued.

There are claims that marijuana has health benefits such as helping with anxiety, insomnia, chronic pain, and epilepsy syndromes. Due to the fact that recreational marijuana is still illegal in most of the country, it can be risky (and illegal) to use. Some industries have begun experimenting with CBD-infused products. These products are THC-free (or less than .3% THC) derivatives of the hemp plant and, unlike marijuana, are legal. Hemp-derived CBD goods are known to relax, relieve anxiety, reduce stress and be therapeutic.[111]

Currently, these goods are difficult to find in mass retailers, and are mostly found in more specialized "whole health" stores. CBD online distributors have a large selection of cannabis-infused products, ranging from food and drinks to body care products containing hemp oil, pet snacks, and a variety of supplemental goods.[112]

The CBD category will set us apart from competitors by introducing new trends and attracting new customers who may be health-conscious, or just curious about the new products. By establishing this category, our typical customers will be able to experience new trends and make active changes in their shopping habits and feelings about our store.

This category will increase traffic and give a more positive overall image of our store as we are recognized for taking a whole-health approach to our customers' lives. We believe that the CBD category has a prominent place in the future of food retail due to its natural health benefits and trendiness to millennials.

Summary of findings:
- Emerging trend
- Growth expected
- Limited sources for customers currently
- Lack of information
- Consumer desire to purchase
- Could obtain "first mover" status

<u>Category Definition</u>

The Category Definition is the first step in the Category Management process, as it defines the selection of the specific stock-keeping units (SKU's) to be carried in the category, it defines the structure or segmentation of the category, and it clearly states which SKU's will not be carried in the category.[113]

Hemp-Derived Cannabidiol Definition:
- This category includes all hemp-derived cannabidiol (CBD), which contain less than .3% THC.
- The category also includes CBD-infused products.
- The category structure is to include segmentation inside food, drinks, personal care, and pet care.
- This category does not include recreational or medical marijuana, or other THC-containing products.

Category Segmentation

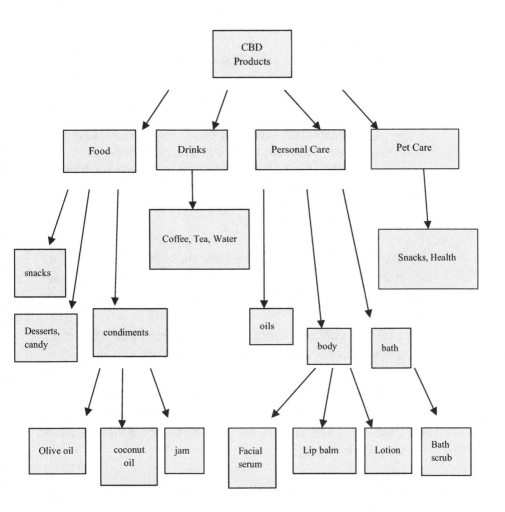

<u>Category Role</u>

Assigning a role to this category establishes the priority and importance related to the overall business, plus assists in determining allocation of resources, including space, assortment, time, focus, etc. Category roles should reflect the following:

- Desired state- Where do you want to be with this category?
- Consumer-orientation- Is the consumer showing they want you to invest heavily in this category?
- Overall fit- Does this category fit in the store's format?
- Understandable- Once you announce its role, will it be understood by the entire company and its suppliers?[114]

Lastly, when determining role, how important is the category to your target consumer, your format as a retailer, your competitors, and what is the overall outlook?

Roles to choose from are: Destination, Preferred, Occasional/Seasonal, and Convenience.

Based upon the rapidly increasing sales outlook, the potential to be "first mover", and overall consumer sentiment, I would suggest hemp-derived Cannabidiol be designated as a Destination category.

Reasoning: This is not a category to "dip your toe into". Either go big or go home! You have the opportunity to be known as the place to find these products, and become a true destination for this customer. If you're going to go in lightly and "see what happens", please just close this book and go back to your desk and watch your competitors kick your butt!

As a Destination category, you are committing to:

- Be the primary provider of these products to the target consumer.
- Help define the category in the marketplace.
- Help define the profile of the retailer in the eyes of the target consumer.
- Lead your competitors in turnover, market share, consumer satisfaction, service level, and return on investment.
- Help lead your company's people, systems, and technological development towards achieving the company's mission, goals, and strategies.

Like I said, go big or go home on this one!

<u>Category Assessment</u>

Normally, in the assessment stage, you want to obtain, organize, and analyze the information necessary to understand the current performance of the category, and identify areas of greatest opportunity for improved results in turnover, profit, sales, market share, etc. For CBD, that will be difficult, if you don't carry it. And, if you do carry it, you probably have no idea if you are maximizing your sales. The category is too new and on too high of a sales trajectory to look at your own numbers. What I would suggest is a type of strengths and weaknesses assessment, to ensure you have a clear understanding of the potential.

Strengths and Opportunities
- CBD has been shown to help with everything from PTSD and anxiety to MS and epilepsy.[115]
- CBD is a natural way to relieve many symptoms.[116]
- Products include: coconut oil, body lotion, face serum, olive oil, jam, bath scrub, cold-brew coffee, sports salve, lip balm, infused water, gummy snacks and dog treats.[117]
- The hemp-CBD market could reach $22 billion by 2022.[118]
- No mass retailers currently in the space, and the biggest opportunity exists there out of all channels for CBD products.[119]
- Some of the biggest distributors are: Entourage Nutritional, US Hemp Wholesale, and HempMeds.[120]

Potential Issues
- There is a stigma on many of the products because they are associated with marijuana.
- Since there is currently less regulation, customers have to educate themselves more.[121]
- People unsure of side effects associated with the usage, and where and when to consume/use.

- CBD products are sold in many formats: natural food stores, cafés, traditional grocery aisles, and even doctor's offices.[122]
- CBD exists in a "legal grey area".[123]
- For suppliers, some get CBD oil cheaper from China, which makes it difficult for locally-sourced suppliers to compete.[124]
- 7/11 is supposed to be carrying Phoenix Tears CBD oils and sprays in the immediate future.[125]

Because CBD products are so new, it is important that thorough research and development goes into the category. By doing this, it will insure that growth, new strategies, and tactics are formed to increase the sales of CBD products. We must look at the target consumer and market the product towards their wants and needs. This will show the customers that the store is updated on the latest trends and will be a competitor to other retailers. The outlook on this market seems promising and with more feedback given by customers, manufacturers and retailers will be able to modify and perfect this category.

Category Scorecard

Once again, it is difficult to produce a current scorecard if you do not carry the products yet. The scorecard normally determines the target objectives to be set, and collaborated upon, with both the retailer and its suppliers. Yes, there is very little information....but, you cannot go into it saying you'll "sell as much as you can". That's not a goal.

Set targets by sub-category, work to ascertain market share information, talk to the trade about who is doing the best in the category, etc. You're going to have to work on this one.

One warning on CBD and CBD-infused products, they are currently on the very expensive range in store retails. Two points on these high retails:

- You'll need to protect your assets. Yes, you might have to use a lockbox for some of these products. They are tiny, and can be upwards of $35 to $135 in retail.
- You'll need to measure tonnage. As more retailers enter this market, precedent says the retail prices will decrease over time as availability increases. Measure tonnage in equivalent units, or you may incorrectly label the category a "failure" because you see deflation for the first few years. Deflation can be expected in this category.

Additional performance measurements for consumers will consist of household penetration, customer satisfaction, transaction size, and loyalty or repeat purchasing. You need to determine if customers are coming back once they purchase the products a few times. It will also be important to understand the "usage cycle", as in how long does it actually take to use a bottle of drops, etc.

Category Strategies

At this step of the process, overall strategic plans are necessary to deliver on the assigned Destination designation, and the accompanying category performance targets. Strategies need to be specified between marketing strategies and product supply strategies. One to make sure you are selling enough, and one to make sure you are making the desired profit rate (including inventory turnover, shrink control, and inventory dollars on hand).

As a Destination category, CBD will need marketing strategies encompassing the following:
- Traffic Building: Focused on drawing traffic to the store and/or into the aisle or category.
- Turf Protecting: You need to establish this category, then build walls (barriers to entry) around it to keep competitors out. You're here to win, remember!
- Transaction Building: Focused on increasing the size of the average transaction in the category, aisle, or total basket size.
- Excitement Creation: Communicate a sense of urgency or opportunity to the consumer.[126]

Notice I did not say "Profit Building". Other than understanding optimum efficiency in your assortment, so you do not waste inventory dollars, a Destination Category is a mindset and a way to build your profile with your customers and inside the industry. If you start out focusing on profit, you'll never know if you've maximized your sales.

For the product supply strategies, keeping in mind this is a Destination Category, you'll need to consider the following:
- Master Data Alignment: This aspect of the process ensures accurate exchange of product, price, and promotional information between the retailer and the

supplier. Retailers and suppliers waste too much time on inaccurate data!

- Ordering: Ensuring the right deliveries are triggered at the right time is essential. If you can hook into Continuous Replenishment (CRP), you should; but, be careful, CRP includes an estimate of item movement- which will be difficult to understand as the sales increase.
- Physical Distribution: The physical product flow from manufacturer to retailer, with a focus on higher service levels, ample stock levels, and lower handling and distribution costs.
- Finance: Financial transactions between suppliers, retailers, stores, etc. A focus on error-free invoices, timely payments, and minimal human interaction, is essential.[127]

As an example, for the four sub-categories (Food, Drinks, Personal Care, and Pet Care), you need to sort your products by strategy. These categories are new, and your format may sell one area of the business better than another format, so the sorting of the products needs to be format-specific.

In general, though, these are the products that will go in each strategy:
- Traffic Building: Products with high share, high household penetration, frequent purchase, and are promotion sensitive.
- Turf Protecting: Known price value products, frequently promoted by target competitor.
- Transaction Building: Products with larger transaction size, and premium products.
- Excitement Creation: New products, seasonal products, rapidly growing products.[128]

If you are a supplier or manufacturer, your job is even more difficult. You are, presumably, producing your products to be sold in all retailers. You will need to develop marketing and product supply strategies by retailer format, as each retailer format has a different target customer, different pricing structure, and different brand message. As a reminder, the dominant formats are:

- Mass merchants: Defined by everyday value-orientation, medium SKU assortment breadth, large footprint and 10-25 mile geographic customer draw.
- Traditional/Promotional: Defined by decent everyday value coupled with highly promotional pricing, extensive SKU assortment breadth, medium footprint, and 5-10 mile geographic customer draw.
- Opening Price Point: Defined by the lowest everyday prices, limited assortment, small footprint, and 1-5 mile geographic customer draw.
- Convenience: Defined by competitive prices on key categories coupled with convenience pricing on non-key categories, large assortment in a few key categories coupled with miniscule assortment in other categories, and a convenience geographic customer draw.
- Specialty: Defined by pricing reflecting the specialization in assortment and sourcing, specialized assortment, and large geographic draw with a smaller focused population.

One additional strategy for CBD products will be around awareness and education. Customers will have some uncertainty with CBD products, due to the fact it is such a new product line. People may not feel comfortable using a product related to marijuana. However, retailers should address people's uncertainties of these products by clearly advertising and messaging on shelves that CBD products do not cause a high and do not have more than .3% THC. It is also important to educate the customers on the uses and purposes of CBD and hemp oil-derived products.

It is important that the sourcing focus be on high quality, trusted brands and a rigorous sourcing policy be followed. Since there are currently no mass retailers of the category, we want to quickly establish the category in our store. This would make us "first movers". Then, we want to integrate traffic-building products, such as CBD drops, at a gross profit rate that will allow growth and establish a base where people will wish to purchase. We will surround the CBD drops, oils, and creams with other CBD products that people would likely try next. This will increase the transactions of these consumers, leading to a higher gross profit rate as well as a growing market and demand of CBD products. These other CBD products surrounding the oil and creams would be transaction builders and would be impulse buys.

For instance, this would include CBD lollipops, gummies, sweets, snacks, and drinks. These goods may not be what the buyer went to the store for, but when they go to buy the main products such oils and drops they will check the goods surrounding those products as well if they look easy to consume or use. We would also try to include limited time only (LTO's) specialty products.

Category Tactics

This step identifies the specific actions to implement the strategies, all while keeping in mind the category's role. In the Category Tactics step, tactics are developed in Assortment, Pricing, Promotion, and Shelf Presentation.

For these steps, the following are the considerations, all while keeping in mind your own specific retailer format:

Assortment

In this step, you are balancing the assortment needs of your consumer with the business objectives of the retailer and suppliers. In this step, you are also establishing criteria for carrying or deleting SKU's. As previously stated, the sourcing criteria for CBD is going to be crucial. Your customers are depending on you to source CBD with integrity.

One of the best sourcing overviews I have found is from Hempfusion. This is not an ad for Hempfusion, only a review of their sourcing communication. This company has done an excellent job of communication their sourcing policies and methods:

Their products include-
"Our Whole Food Hemp Complex, comprised of phytonutrient dense Hemp stalk and seed oil, clove, black pepper fruit, sunflower oils, and key hemp derived phytocompounds:
- Key Hemp Phytocompounds
- Omega Rich fatty Acids
- Terpenes
- Phospholipids
- Other Phytonutrients"[129]

Hempfusion then relates "To ensure purity, safety, and content uniformity, all Hempfusion raw materials are 3rd party tested by Independent Laboratories for: pesticides, herbicides, residual solvents, heavy metals, fatty acid profile. Phytonutrient profile, key hemp phytocompounds, terpenes.

Our products contain no GMO's, soy, gluten, wheat, milk, dairy, eggs, shellfish, magnesium stearate, artificial colors, artificial flavors, chemical processing aids."[130]

And then, to add one more point of validity to their products, Hempfusion adds "All Hemp grown under European Eco-Farming practices, certified European non-GMO hemp, DNA verified to be legally compliant with all US federal laws, extracted using only clean and solvent free CO2 extraction, vegan, manufactured in an ISO 9000 compliant and HACCP certified facility, and allergen free source (FALCPA)."[131]

No, I have no idea if they do everything they say. I'm only using it as an example of the clarity needed to provide assurances to the customers that you are doing your due diligence.

The appropriate assortment tactics should only be decided after considering the following factors:
✓ Variety Needs of Target Consumer
- o What does the Consumer Decision Tree indicate?
- o What are the minimum coverage levels for variety to meet consumer needs?
✓ Current Variety Image
- o How does the current variety compare to competition?
- o Who is perceived to be the current category variety leader? Why?

- ✓ Marketing Strategy
  - o What level of variety is consistent with the retailer's overall marketing strategy?
- ✓ Category Role and Strategies
  - o What level of variety is consistent with the category role and strategies?
- ✓ Cost/Benefit of Different Variety Levels
  - o What are the opportunities?
  - o How "long" is the tail? (e.g., last 2% of turnover comes from last 20% of SKUs)
  - o What is the minimum performance acceptable to carry an item?
  - o What is the gain required to offset the cost on inventory, space, and administration?
  - o What is variety and what is duplication?
- ✓ Product Acceptance and Deletion Criteria
  - o What criteria should be used for accepting and rejecting products given the category role and strategies?
- ✓ Supplier Capabilities
  - o Can category suppliers support tactical decisions?[132]

Pricing

Tactics in this area determine the prices the retailer offers to consumers for the products carried in the category. As with all decisions in all tactical areas, these decisions must be based on the category's role, target performance measures, and category strategies as well as on an understanding of consumer and competitive behavior. The key tactical choices that exist in the area of pricing are:

- ✓ Value Provided to Target Consumer

- How important is pricing in the value offered to consumers in this category?
- How price sensitive are target consumers?
- Which products are the most price-sensitive in the category?

✓ Current Price Image
- What does the category assessment reveal?
- How does the pricing compare to competition?
- Who is perceived to be the category price leader? Why?
- What are the key price image items of the category?

✓ Marketing Strategy
- What pricing is consistent with the company's overall pricing and marketing strategy (e.g., high/low, EDLP, etc.)?

✓ Category Role and Strategies
- What pricing is consistent with the category role and strategies?

✓ Cost/Benefit of Various Pricing Options
- Will price increase/decrease significantly impact category turnover and profit?
- Are private label items priced correctly in relation to supplier-branded products?
- How should new items be priced?
- What are likely competitor responses to any price changes?[133]

Promotion

Tactics in this area determine the retailer promotions to be offered to the consumer in the category. The promotion tactics define the criteria for using various vehicles (advertised features, displays, sampling, contests, etc.) to promote the components of the category (e.g., segments, brands, SKUs, etc.) to execute the category strategies. Specific promotional tactics are defined, and the final output of this step is a detailed calendar of promotional events linked to the achievement of the category strategies. Promotional tactics play an especially important role in the Category Business Plan because they are the main source of creative selling ideas.[134]

The questions include:
- ✓ Marketing Strategy
  - o What promotions are consistent with the company's overall marketing strategy?
  - o How will the target consumer respond to various promotions?
  - o What is the promotion activity of competitors in this category?
  - o How will competitors respond to various promotions?
  - o What impact does promotion have on the image of the item, category, and retailer?
- ✓ Category Role and Strategies
  - o Which promotions best deliver the assigned role and execute the category strategies?
  - o What criteria are most important for choosing the right promotions?
- ✓ Cost/Benefit of Various Promotions
  - o How well do promotions work in the category? Do they increase turnover? Market share? Profit for the category? How much do they cannibalize existing results?
  - o Does the promotion attract new consumers and do they buy other products as well as the promoted item?
  - o Which promotions build consumer loyalty?

- o Which promotions create unfavorable purchasing behavior and erode brand and store equity?
- o What do various promotional options cost? What return on investment does a promotion generate?

Shelf Presentation

Tactics in this area determine how the category will be presented to consumers at the point of sale. Some of the key decisions made in this step are the criteria used for managing shelf space (in the category, sub-categories, segments and SKUs), category location in store and in aisle, category layout, on-shelf service levels (e.g., minimum days of supply, case pack out, etc.), and specific sub-category/ segment and SKU space allocation.

The decisions must also reflect important strategic issues, such as the best location for the category in the store and the best overall flow of products on the shelf. Tactical decisions are extremely important because consumers primarily see the result of Category Management at the shelf level.[135]

These decisions include:
- ✓ Target Consumer
  - o Is the shelf presentation logical and "shoppable" based on the needs and/or wants of the target consumers and how they make purchase decisions in the category (the Consumer Decision Tree)?
- ✓ Competitive Positioning
  - o Does the shelf presentation help highlight key points of competitive differentiation sought by the retailer?
- ✓ Marketing Strategy

- o Is the desired variety image communicated and reinforced by the shelf presentation?
- ✓ Category Role and Strategies
  - o What shelf presentation is consistent with the category role and strategies?
- ✓ Cost/ Benefit of Various Shelf Presentation Options
  - o How are operational issues considered (e.g. cost of restocking)?
  - o What impact will a particular location within the store have on category sales and profit?
  - o What impact will a particular category layout have on category sales and profit?
  - o Does the shelf presentation help the retailer implement its customer service strategy at store level?

CBD and CBD-Infused

In a traditional store format-

- ✓ We will have our own section of CBD goods, and it will be designed similar to an organic goods aisle or a gluten-free aisle.
- ✓ The aisle will be located near organic goods, as well as health and beauty care; and will likely be closer to outside aisles rather than in the center of the store.
- ✓ It will be divided by Food, Drinks, Personal Care, and Pet Care.
- ✓ Sweets and treats next to each other, followed by candies, drinks and drink mixes, condiments, then supplements, body care, and homeopathic pet treatments in their own segmented section with signage representing where the products are and the benefits associated.
- ✓ We will be selling goods including sweets such as cookies and brownies, chocolates and chocolate bars, hard candies, pure CBD drops, lollipops, and a variety of gummies.

- ✓ The drinks we will sell include coffees, teas, and other mixes like fruit punches.
- ✓ There will also be frozen treats, including ice cream and frozen yogurts.
- ✓ There will be body care, like lotions, washes, and face care.
- ✓ Then there will be pet care products such as treats and pet supplements for homeopathic pet treatment.

Other tactics:
- ✓ Our category will likely have a selection of products for customers to try. We will focus on selling the high quality natural products and brands.
- ✓ There will be limited variety of each item, but we will have plenty of ways for people to experience CBD goods in their lifestyles.
- ✓ We intend to integrate new products into monthly flyers in our stores and send out coupons to our usual customers to increase the growth of the market.
- ✓ The signage in the aisle is important to our promotion of the products, because we want people to be informed and understand the usage of CBD, the side effects, etc.

Plan Implementation

This step in the Category Management process develops a specific implementation schedule and assigns responsibilities for completing all tactical actions. The potential benefits of Category Management lie in the implementation of Category Business Plans. These plans are of little value if they are not implemented, or are implemented poorly.

The key components of plan implementation are:
- o Approval Process
- o Assigning Responsibilities
- o Scheduling

Plan Approval Process

The criteria for approval of a Category Business Plan should include:

Strategic Fit- Management should be certain that the Category Business Plan is consistent with the company's overall strategy.

Target Performance Impact- An important aspect of the approval process is to confirm the projected impact of the plan on the category performance targets.

Resource Allocation- The approval process should "sign-off" on any additional resources requested by the retailer and the supplier, especially if the plan requests additional resources beyond what has already been allocated (e.g., a new type of cooler, more shelf space, more promotion activity, etc.).

Impact on Other Areas- If the Category Business Plan impacts other functional areas of a retailer's or supplier's business, the approval process must recognize and manage this issue. For example, will the promotional tactics within the plan have any implications for the supplier's marketing function? Will the retailer's store engineering department be impacted by plans to relocate the category within the store? Answers to these types of questions should have been provided in the development of the Category Business Plan, but it is important that management agree to manage these issues as part of the plan approval process.

Assignment of Responsibilities

This step involves assigning each tactical action required in the plan to individuals for execution. Retailers typically assign tasks to the category manager, senior management and functions throughout their system (e.g., store operation, logistics, information systems and finance).

Suppliers may assign tasks to the account executive, senior management, product supply, information systems, customer service and, frequently, marketing or product development. For example, in order to implement the assortment tactics it may be necessary to authorize several new products, discontinue stocking some items, revise the planogram and reset store shelves. The implementation plan will assign each of these tasks to individuals in the supplier's and retailer's organization.

Implementation Scheduling

This step involves the development of timelines and milestones for the tasks, which have been assigned. An essential tool for quality implementation is a detailed implementation calendar. The calendar includes dates for completion of all tactical actions, as well as dates for reviewing plan progress.

Implementation
Success Requirements

- Top management commitment to implementation
- Detailed Implementation Plan
- Involvement of Store Operations
- Category Plans must be "store relevant"
- Review and redesign current implementation processes
- Assign specific responsibility and performance measures at HQ and store levels

136

Category Review

The final step in the Category Management process is to conduct an ongoing review and measurement of the progress of the plan towards the category role and target performance measures, and to modify the plan as appropriate. Category Business Plans are typically annual plans. Their results should he extensively reviewed annually and less extensive reviews should be conducted at least on a quarterly basis.[137]

CBD is a rapidly growing category, and should be subjected to ongoing reviews. I would call for abbreviated category reviews every three months. Supplier reviews should happen even more frequently.

Some of the key questions when measuring the category's performance are:

✓ How often should the Category Business Plan be evaluated? This will depend upon the category and its role. Destination categories tend to be evaluated more frequently.
✓ What role does the retailer play in measuring the category's progress? The supplier? This will depend upon the information capabilities of each party.
✓ What format should this measurement reporting follow? A common review format for all plans should be developed to eliminate the confusion and complexity created by having different formats and measures. This format should contain, at a minimum, a comparison of actual vs. target performance levels, an explanation of any variances and actions to be taken to modify the plan's implementation as a result of these variances.

This sounds like fun, let's do it!

That's the right attitude! You have everything laid out for you: the reason to pursue, the clarity of which segment to pursue, the fact that you can be "first mover" in a massive growth-projected segment of our business, you have customers already asking for it, and you've been given a process through which you can make your plan. All you need now is the desire to beat your competitors to the punch!

Like I said, don't "dip your toe" into CBD. It's going to take an all-out effort to win. Go big or go home! And, if you're thinking of opening THC dispensaries, that is awesome! You are to be commended for being on trend and wanting to be ahead of the customer!

Thanks,

Dr. Z

Endnotes

[1] Shipmah, Matt. (2019). Is hemp the same thing as marijuana? https://phys.org/news/2019-02-hemp-marijuana.html

[2] The Thistle. (2000). The People's History. https://www.mit.edu/~thistle/v13/2/history.html

[3] Ibid.

[4] Ibid.

[5] https://www.cancer.gov/publications/dictionaries/cancer-terms/def/psychoactive-substance

[6] Ren et al. (2019). The Origins of Cannabis Smoking. Science Advances 12 Jun 2019:Vol. 5, no. 6, eaaw1391DOI: 10.1126/sciadv.aaw1391. https://advances.sciencemag.org/content/5/6/eaaw1391

[7] What is the difference between opioids and cannabis? https://arborswellness.com/blog/what-is-the-difference-between-opioids-and-cannabis/

[8] https://americanmarijuana.org/marijuana-statistics/

[9] Ibid.

[10] Ibid.

[11] Ibid.

[12] https://americanmarijuana.org/cbd-for-pain-2020-study-of-1453-consumers/

[13] https://disa.com/map-of-marijuana-legality-by-state

[14] https://www.statista.com/statistics/737849/share-americans-age-group-smokes-marijuana/

[15] https://www.leafly.com/news/science-tech/meet-bliss-molecule-anandamide-cannabinoid

[16] Ibid.

[17] https://pubchem.ncbi.nlm.nih.gov/compound/Anandamide

[18] https://www.drugabuse.gov/publications/research-reports/marijuana/how-does-marijuana-produce-its-effects

[19] Ibid.

[20] https://www.vice.com/en_us/article/yvxe3m/whats-the-deal-with-greening-out

[21] https://www.leafly.com

[22] https://weedmaps.com/learn/dictionary/flower/

[23] https://weedmaps.com/learn/dictionary/bowl/

[24] https://www.leafly.com/news/cannabis-101/glossary-of-cannabis-terms

[25] https://www.analyticalcannabis.com/articles/the-difference-between-cannabinoids-and-terpenes-311502

[26] Ibid.

[27] https://www.history.com/news/the-hazy-history-of-420

[28] https://kushfly.com/blog/happy-710-heres-what-710-oil-day-is-all-about/

[29] https://www.medicalnewstoday.com/articles/indica-vs-sativa#physical-differences-in-strains

[30] https://www.marijuanadoctors.com/resources/cbd-thc-ratios/

[31] https://wayofleaf.com/education/top-cannabinoids-and-what-they-do

[32] Ibid.

[33] Ibid.

[34] Ibid.

[35] Ibid.

[36] https://www.newyorker.com/magazine/2017/10/30/the-family-that-built-an-empire-of-pain

[37] CBD Origin (2018). https://cbdorigin.com/is-cbd-legal/

[38] CBD Origin (2017). https://cbdorigin.com/cbd-isolate-vs-full-spectrum-cbd/

[39] Made by Hemp (2019). CBD Regulations for Six Top Sports Organizations. https://madebyhemp.com/cbd-and-sports/

[40] https://finance.yahoo.com/news/2020-olympics-athletes-cbd-213524019.html

[41] Made by Hemp (2019). CBD Regulations for Six Top Sports Organizations. https://madebyhemp.com/cbd-and-sports/

[42] http://www.ncaa.org/sport-science-institute/topics/2020-21-ncaa-banned-substances

[43] https://www.nutraingredients-usa.com/Article/2020/03/16/CBD-paves-way-for-marijuana-leniency-in-NFL#

[44] Made by Hemp (2019). CBD Regulations for Six Top Sports Organizations. https://madebyhemp.com/cbd-and-sports/

[45] Ibid.

[46] Ibid.

[47] Ibid.

[48] Ibid.

[49] https://hempindustrydaily.com/fda-reissues-post-on-recall-of-lead-contaminated-cbd-oil-from-florida-manufacturer/

[50] https://www.marijuanamoment.net/fda-updates-congress-on-cbd-product-labelling-accuracy/

[51] https://www.foodbusinessnews.net/articles/16405-fda-uncovers-mislabeled-cbd-products

[52] https://www.cbdoil.org/sunsoil-cbd-review/

[53] Smith, Cooper (2019). Addiction Center. https://www.addictioncenter.com/opiates/opioid-epidemic/

[54] Ibid.

[55] Sherter, Alain (2019). New York State Files Fraud Charges Against Purdue Pharma and Sackler Family. CBS News. https://www.cbsnews.com/news/purdue-pharma-lawsuit-sackler-family-new-york-state-opioids/

[56] Smith, Cooper (2019). Addiction Center. https://www.addictioncenter.com/opiates/opioid-epidemic/

[57] Ibid.

[58] Ibid.

[59] Hempfusion.com (2018).

[60] Encyclopedia Brittanica (2018). https://www.britannica.com/science/homeostasis

[61] Zwanka, Russell (2018). CBD Dreams. KDP Publishing.

[62] CBD Origin (2018). https://medium.com/cbd-origin/the-endocannabinoid-system-everything-you-need-to-know-1c38a648cafb

[63] Ibid

[64] Ibid

[65] Brightfield Group (2017 June). Summary Report; Understanding Cannabidiol. In Statista - The Statistics Portal. Retrieved April 20, 2019, https://www-statista-com.ezproxy.siena.edu/study/50238/cannabidiol-survey-on-users-and-market-2017/

[66] Kuhl, L. (2019, January 24). Take a look at three companies best positioned to take on the $22 billion CBD industry. Retrieved April 18, 2019, from https://www.potnetwork.com/news/take-look-three-companies-best-positioned-take-22-billion-cbd-industry

[67] Ibid.

[68] Hudak, J. (2018, December 13). The Farm Bill, hemp legalization and the status of CBD: An explainer. Retrieved April 19, 2019, from https://www.brookings.edu/blog/fixgov/2018/12/14/the-farm-bill-hemp-and-cbd-explainer/

[69] DEA.gov. (n.d.). Drug Scheduling. Retrieved from https://www.dea.gov/drug-scheduling

[70] HelloMD. "Understanding Cannabidiol CBD Industry report - Hello MD - Brightfield group https://www.hellomd.com

[71] Shute, Nancy. "The Science of CBD Lags behind Its Marketing." Science News, vol. 195, no. 6, Mar. 2019, p. 2. https://www.sciencenews.org/article/science-cbd-lags-behind-its-marketing

[72] Pisanti, S, Malfitano, A, Lamberti, et al.: State of the art and new challenges for therapeutic applications. Pharmacology & Therapeutics OL February 2017 Pg. 133-150. Retrieved April 20, 2019 from Science Direct. 1. https://www.sciencedirect.com/science/article/pii/S0163725817300657?via%3Dihub

[73] Bible, A. (2019, March). WHAT'S THE DEAL WITH CBD? This plant compound found in marijuana may be able to help drive gains by wiping out pain and boosting recovery. Joe Weider's Muscle & Fitness, 80(3), 124+. Retrieved from http://link.galegroup.com.ezproxy.siena.edu:2048/apps/doc/A578157276/HRCA?u=nysl_ca_siena&sid=HRCA&xid=da2f0219

[74] Abacus Health Products. "CBDMEDIC Launches Topical Pain Relief Medications." PR Newswire: Press Release Distribution, Targeting, Monitoring and Marketing, 27 Mar. 2019, www.prnewswire.com/news-releases/cbdmedic-launches-topical-pain-relief-medications-300819477.html.

[75] Campbell, Fiona A; Tramèr, Martin R; Carroll, Dawn; Reynolds, John; Moore, Andrew; McQuay, Henry. Are cannabinoids an effective and safe treatment option in the management of pain? A qualitative systematic review BMJ 2001; 323 :13

[76] Hempfusion.com.(2018).https://hempfusion.com/executive-team/

[77] Wang, Tongtong; Collet, Jean-Paul; Shapiro, Stan; Ware, Mark. Adverse effects of medical cannabinoids: a systematic review. CMAJ Jun 2008, 178 (13) 1669-1678; DOI: 10.1503/cmaj.071178

[78] "CBD User Manual." Project CBD: Medical Marijuana & Cannabinoid Science, www.projectcbd.org/guidance/cbd-users-manual

[79] Cadena, Aaron. "5 Ways CBD Is Smashing People's Perspectives of Cannabis." Medium.com, Medium, 23 May 2018, www.cbdorigin//medium.com/cbd-origin/5-ways-cbd-is-smashing-peoples-perspectives-of-cannabis-8fd733b19dc9

[80] Taylor, J. (2018, October 15). What Is CBD? Here's What to Know About Cannabidiol. https://www.menshealth.com/health/a22126593/what-is-cbd-oil

[81] Devash, M. (2019, April 23). Everything You Need to Know About the CBD Beauty Trend. Retrieved from https://www.allure.com/story/cbd-oil-in-beauty-products

[82] Grinspoon, P. (2018, August 24). Cannabidiol (CBD) - what we know and what we don't. Retrieved from https://www.health.harvard.edu/blog/cannabidiol-cbd-what-we-know-and-what-we-dont-2018082414476

[83] What CBD does for skin acne. (n.d.). Retrieved from https://benicepaper.com/

[84] CBD Skin Care Market Insights: Growth Factors, Market Drivers, Segmentations, Key Players, Analysis & Forecast by 2027. (n.d.). Retrieved from https://honestversion.com/cbd-skin-care-market-insights-growth-factors-market-drivers-segmentations-key-players-analysis-forecast-by-2027/

[85] Oláh, A., Szabó-Papp, J., Szabó, P. T., Stott, C., Zouboulis, C. C., Bíró, T., & Arnold Markovics. (2016, June 15). Differential effectiveness of selected non-psychotropic phytocannabinoids on human sebocyte functions implicates their introduction in dry/seborrhoeic skin and acne treatment. Retrieved from https://onlinelibrary.wiley.com/doi/epdf/10.1111/exd.13042

[86] Grinspoon, P. (2018, August 24). Cannabidiol (CBD) - what we know and what we don't. Retrieved from https://www.health.harvard.edu/blog/cannabidiol-cbd-what-we-know-and-what-we-dont-2018082414476

[87] Greb, Alexandra, and Birgit Puschner. "Cannabinoid Treats as Adjunctive Therapy for Pets: Gaps in Our Knowledge." Toxicology Communications, vol. 2, no. 1, 2018, pp. 10–14., doi:10.1080/24734306.2018.1434470.

[88] Kogan, Lori, et al. "Consumers' Perceptions of Hemp Products for Animals ." Consumers' Perception of Hemp Products For Animals , vol. 42, 2016, doi: 10.18411/lj-31-10-2016-1-11.

[89] AVMA. "A Sign of the Times: Medical Marijuana Use and Veterinary Medicine." Atwork.avma.org, American Veterinary Medical Association, 15 July 2013, atwork.avma.org/2013/07/15/a-sign-of-the-times-medical-marijuana-use-and-veterinary-medicine/.

[90] Marquiss, Nick. "Honest Paws." Honest Paws, Honest Paws, 29 Jan. 2018, www.honestpaws.com/pages/about-us.

[91] Pet Releaf. "Your Guide To Pet Releaf's Most Frequently Asked Questions." Pet CBD Oil - CBD Products —, 9 Apr. 2019, petreleaf.com/others/faqs.

[92] Mull, Amanda. "The Sad News About CBD Cupcakes." The Atlantic, Atlantic Media Company, 17 Jan. 2019, www.theatlantic.com/health/archive/2019/01/cbd-food/580483/

[93] "CBD Infused Candy, CBD Chocolate, CBD Soda." Cannabinoid Creations, cannabinoidcreations.com/.

[94] Foodnavigator-Usa.com. "SPECIAL FEATURE: What Is the Regulatory Status of CBD in Food and Beverage Products?" Foodnavigator, www.foodnavigator-usa.com/Article/2018/10/11/SPECIAL-FEATURE-What-is-the-regulatory-status-of-CBD-in-food-and-beverage-products.

[95] LaVito, Angelica. "FDA Plans First Public Hearings on Legalizing CBD Foods in April." CNBC, CNBC, 27 Feb. 2019, www.cnbc.com/2019/02/27/fda-plans-first-public-hearings-on-legalizing-cbd-foods-in-april.html

[96] Doheny, Kathleen. "Marijuana, Hemp, CBD Oil: What's Legal and Where." WebMD,WebMD, 8 Jan. 2019,www.webmd.com/pain-management/news/20190108/marijuana-hemp-cbd-whats-legal-and-where.

[97] Gold, Michael. "New York City Cracks Down on CBD Edibles, Saying the Cannabis Derivative Is Unsafe." The New York Times, The New York Times, 5 Feb. 2019, www.nytimes.com/2019/02/05/nyregion/cbd-food-nyc-restaurants.html.

[98] Williams, Alex. "Why Is CBD Everywhere?" The New York Times, The New York Times, 27 Oct. 2018, www.nytimes.com/2018/10/27/style/cbd-benefits.html.

[99] Ibid

[100] Ibid

[101] Medical News Today (2017). https://www.medicalnewstoday.com/articles/248423.php

[102] CBD Origin (2018). https://medium.com/cbd-origin/the-endocannabinoid-system-everything-you-need-to-know-1c38a648cafb

[103] Ibid

[104] Ibid

[105] "Honest Weight Fresh News." Honest Weight Food Co-Op. www.honestweight.coop/page/honest-weight-fresh-news-287/news/cbd-what-it-is-where-you-can-find-it--why-you-should-try-it-83.html.

[106] Walker, Matt (2019). Ted Talk: Sleep is your superpower. https://www.ted.com/talks/matt_walker_sleep_is_your_superpower

[107] https://www.supermarketnews.com/cbd/podcast-nielsen-s-rick-maturo-says-us-cbd-market-could-top-25-billion

[108] Zwanka, Russell; Harris, Brian (2016). Category Management Principles. KDP Publishing, 978-1533452498

[109] Ibid.

[110] Statista (2018). https://www.statista.com/statistics/760498/total-us-cbd-sales/

[111] Harvard Health (2018). https://www.health.harvard.edu/blog/cannabidiol-cbd-what-we-know-and-what-we-dont-2018082414476

[112] Cannabinoid Creations (2018). https://cannabinoidcreations.com

[113] Zwanka and Harris. Category Management Principles.

[114] Ibid.

[115] Garber-Paul, Elisabeth. "Exclusive: New Report Predicts CBD Market Will Hit $22 Billion by 2022." Rolling Stone, Rolling Stone, 11 Sept. 2018, www.rollingstone.com/culture/culture-news/new-study-cbd-market-22-billion-2022-722852/.

[116] Ibid.

[117] Mallenbaum, Carly. "What Is CBD? And Why Is the Cannabis-Derived Ingredient on the Rise for Wellness Products?" USA Today, USA Today, 21 Oct. 2018, www.usatoday.com/story/life/wellness/2018/10/05/cbd-cannabis-marijuana-therapy-wellness-food-pets/1459285002/

[118] Garber-Paul, Elisabeth.

[119] Ibid.

[120] Weimert, Kelly. "The Ultimate Guide to CBD Oil Distributors." Cannabis FN, 7 Feb. 2018, www.cannabisfn.com/ultimate-guide-cbd-oil-distributors/

[121] Naturally Splendid, Inc. "CBD Market Estimated to Grow to $2.1B by 2020, Report Finds 'Hemp-Derived CBD Is Estimated to Account for $450 Million.'" Naturally Splendid, Inc., 5 Jan. 2017, naturallysplendid.com/resources/2017/01/cbd-market-estimated-grow-2-1b-2020-report-finds-hemp-derived-cbd-estimated-account-450-million/

[122] Garber-Paul, Elisabeth.

[123] Ibid.

[124] Naturally Splendid.

[125] Hemp Industry Daily. "CBD Manufacturer Signs Deal to Get Product in 7-Eleven Stores." Hemp Industry Daily, Hemp Industry Daily, 6 June 2018, hempindustrydaily.com/7-eleven-cbd-products-4500-stores-by-year-end/

[126] Zwanka and Harris. Category Management Principles.

[127] Ibid.

[128] Ibid.

[129] Hempfusion (2018).

[130] Ibid.

[131] Ibid.

[132] Zwanka and Harris. Category Management Principles.

[133] Ibid.

[134] Ibid.

[135] Ibid.

[136] Ibid.

[137] Ibid.

Made in United States
North Haven, CT
27 January 2023

31669406R00059